Application of Webometrics on Modern Information Research

By
Dr. Ashok Pal
Arindam Sarkar
Sanjoy Kar

Ess Ess Publications
New Delhi

Application of Webometrics on Modern Information Research

ISBN : 978-93-87698-31-4

Price : Rs. 500/-

First Published 2021

Published by:
Ess Ess Publications
4831/24, Ansari Road,
Darya Ganj,
New Delhi-110 002.
INDIA
Phones: 23260807, 41563444
Fax: 41563334
E-mail: info@essessreference.com
www.essessreference.com

Cover Design by *Patch Creative Unit*

Printed and bound in India

Contents

Acknowledgements

We would like to convey our sincere thanks to our respected teachers of the Departments of Library and Information Science of Jadavpur University and Vidyasagar University for their constant efforts in encouraging us to move forward with our innovative thoughts. We would also like to give hearty thanks to our near and dear ones for their support. Two case studies of this book "Webometric Mapping of Indian Tourism Sites" and "Webometric Analysis of Indian Banks" have been published earlier in the e-journal Library Philosophy and Practice. These research works have been included in this book for representing the wide application of webometrics research in the modern world. Last but not the least a big thanks to all of our well wishers without whose blessings and best wishes this work would not have been completed.

Dr. Ashok Pal
Arindam Sarkar
Sanjoy Kar

Preface

In the Web dominated 21st century not a single sphere of life can be witnessed, where web has not spread its wings. Whether it is education or health or defence or space research or engineering or agriculture or sports or even in the banking or industrial sector web has established its supremacy. Web has made a man a global citizen. Now the obvious question is how to measure this vast web phenomena and the solution is a kind of quantitative metrical analysis which is popularly known as webometric analysis of websites. This webometrics is concerned with measuring different aspects of the Web like websites, web pages, parts of web pages, words in web pages, page size, domain or page authority, descriptor tags, hyperlinks, web search engine results and the like. Be it a content analysis of websites or Web Impact Factor analysis or Search engine optimization analysis or Web link structure analysis, all are part of this larger family named Webometrics Research. This book through its different chapters has figured out various types of webometrics analysis. The real life examples which have been represented in the chapters of this book will definitely help the students and scholars to have a clear picture of how to conduct a webometrics research.

Dr. Ashok Pal
Arindam Sarkar
Sanjoy Kar

1
A Brief Introduction to Webometrics

Tomas Almind and Peter Ingwersen's epoch making article in 1997 first introduced the term *webometrics*. It heralded the birth of a new subject domain which reflected web as a vital source for measuring documents and information. Though cybermetrics and webometrics emerged almost at the same time cybermetrics was given more general phenomena by referring to non-web Internet research, such as email or newsgroup studies, in addition to web research and webometrics was defined as "the study of web-based phenomena using quantitative techniques and drawing upon informetric methods" (Björneborn & Ingwersen, 2004).

In this 21st century not a single sphere of life can be witnessed, where web has not spread its wings. Whether it is education or health or defence or space research or engineering or agriculture or sports or even in the banking or industrial sector web has established its supremacy. Web has emerged as the important repository of all sorts of information. In this age of information easily available information (in its different shapes like books, articles, web documents, reports, theses and so on) through the mirror of web has also conquered thousands of hearts. Web has made a man a global citizen. Today any institution or any person can showcase their web existence as well as can communicate with the larger audience through their respective websites. Webpage is the basic unit of this web presence (i.e. website). Now the obvious question which occurs in our mind is how to measure this vast web phenomena and the solution is a kind of quantitative metrical analysis which is popularly known as webometric analysis of websites. This webometrics is concerned with measuring different aspects of the Web like websites, web pages, parts of web pages, words in web pages, page size, domain or page authority, descriptor tags, hyperlinks, web search engine results and the like. Webometric analysis of websites can be done through the content analysis of websites, calculating different types of Web Impact Factors, web citation analysis, designing the pattern of hyperlinks or through measuring search engine optimization. Though content analysis mainly focuses on the qualitative aspect of website analysis, this is doubtlessly vital to investigate the impact of a website. Thelwall (2009) also emphasizes on the mixing of both qualitative and quantitative aspects of website analysis.

Björneborn and Ingwersen (2004) opined that there is a connection between bibliometrics, informetrics and webometrics. To them webometrics is "the study of the quantitative aspects of the construction and use of information resources, structures and technologies on the web drawing on bibliometric and informetric approaches". This definition thus covers quantitative aspects of both the construction side and the usage side of the web embracing four main areas of present webometric research:

1. Web page content analysis;
2. Web link structure analysis;

3. Web usage analysis (including log files of users' searching and browsing behaviour);
4. Web technology analysis (including search engine performance).

Though this subject domain has its origin in the quantitative analysis studies like bibliometrics and informetrics, webometrics has its focus on the metrical analysis of the web. Thelwall's effort of defining webometrics culminates in the following words "the study of web-based content with primarily quantitative methods for social science research goals using techniques that are not specific to one field of study." This definition sets webometrics free from informetrics which is mainly the quantitative research centered on measuring information and this definition of webometrics also gives it wide social science audience while excluding field-specific methods such as linguistic analyses of online language. The restriction to social science goals also excludes purely mathematical analyses of web-based content. Although early webometrics research explicitly analyzed the web as a document network, the above definition does not rule out analyses of web page contents. Finally, the definition is broad enough to encompass research by people who would not describe themselves as webometricians but as researchers using web measurements in other fields (Thelwall, 2009). Whereas Björneborn and Ingwersen emphasize on the informetric and bibliometric origin of webometrics, Thelwall focuses on the value that webometrics could provide to the wider social sciences.

Webometrics research though had its focus primarily on the field of education as is seen in the analysis of the websites of academic institutions, in analysing the websites of different sectors like tourism, politics, banking and industrial sector, sports fraternity, government and non-government organizations and so on webometrics research also plays its part. To represent this variety of webometrics research, representing various web analysis techniques as well as different types of application areas, five meticulous case studies have been represented in this book.

REFERENCES

- Björneborn, L., & Ingwersen, P. (2004). Toward a basic framework for webometrics. *Journal of the American Society for Information Science and Technology, 55*(14), 1216-1227.
- Thelwall, M. (2009). Introduction to webometrics: Quantitative web research for the social sciences. Morgan & Claypool.

2

Websites of Institutes of Eminence in India : A Webometric Study

ABSTRACT

"Institute of Eminence" is UGC's venture of taking the popular educational institutions of India into world level prominence. Web Impact Factor (WIF), Search Engine Optimization (SEO) etc. improve the visibility of a website's presence in online environment. The present study predominantly focuses on the WIFs and SEO of the 18 Institutes of Eminence websites. This quantitative analysis of the selected websites upholds some of the qualities of these websites. While according to Simple Web Impact Factor (SWIF), Internal-link Web Impact Factor (IWIF) and External- link Web Impact Factor (EWIF) ranking website of Jamia Hamdard (JH), New Delhi, holds the numerouno status. IIT Delhi website has the best Indian ranking i.e. 390 and Delhi University website has the best global ranking i.e. 3437. IIT Bombay has the heaviest webpage and i.e.

2.2 MB and consequently it has the worst load time of 63.53seconds. IIT Delhi website and Jadavpur University websites boast of little load time of 0.47 and 1.01 seconds respectively. Jadavpur University website has the highest domain authority score of 53 and IIT Madras has the highest page authority score of 57.

Keywords: Institutes of Eminence, Web Impact Factor, WIF, Search Engine Optimization, SEO, Popularity Rank, Link Mapping

INTRODUCTION

Twenty first century has witnessed a remarkable growth in the field of information and communication technologies (ICT). Not a single sphere of life has escaped from its fast growing coverage. Education is a field where ICT has its immense influence. When it comes to the web presence of an educational institution its weightage is measured through its website's quality. In India, the UGC, in its 542nd meeting held on 02nd August 2019 has considered the reports of the Empowered Expert Committee (EEC) appointed by Government under the Chairmanship of Shri N. Gopalaswami recommending 15 public institutions and 15 private institutions for giving the status of Institutions of Eminence. At the outset the UGC has selected only 10 public and 10 private institutions, after examining the list of 30 institutions (15 public and 15 private) using transparent and verifiable criteria. Since the thrust of the scheme is to prepare institutions for the global rankings, no existing institution which has not figured in any of the global/national ranks shall be recommended for the Institute of Eminence status (Press Information Bureau, 2019). The present paper attempts to analyse and evaluate the websites of the Institutes of Eminence on the basis of Web Impact Factor (WIF), Search Engine Optimization (SEO) and link topology designing. Mapping of the links using SocSciBot and Pajek software is also the forte of this paper.

REVIEW OF LITERATURE

Babu, Jeyshankar and Nageswara Rao (2013) examined 40 central universities websites in India and also develops a novel network diagram showing link structures between web nodes in webometric analysis.

Jakopee, Hoare and Riordan (2012) carried out a comparative analysis of hyperlink connectivity between higher education and research sites within two European countries. A categorization of both Ireland's and Croatia's educational and research domains and sub-domains served as input to a customized web crawler to compute relevant connectivity measures. Trends and differences in both counties' interconnections were observed.

Jalal, Biswas and Mukhopadhyay (2010) studied the webometric analysis of central universities in India. They used Yahoo and Google search engines using special query syntax. Result revealed that University of Delhi achieved top rank and Sikkim University occupied the last.

OBJECTIVES

The objectives of the study are as follows:

- To calculate the simple, internal-link and external-link web impact factors of selected websites.
- To show the domain extension percentage of the websites.
- To find out the global and Indian popularity ranking of the websites.
- To analyze the websites of selected institutes on the basis of SEO.
- To design the link mapping of the websites.

METHODOLOGY

Data have been collected from the websites of selected educational institutes in India. Data have been collected during 15 to 20 September, 2019. For calculating three types of WIFs (simple, self-link or internal-link and external link WIF) first the number of links has been counted from a link analyser tool named CleverStat (http://cleverstat.com/link-analyzer). For calculating the number of webpages of a particular website "site:domain name" syntax has been used (Sarkar and Pal, 2018). On the basis of these, the formula of calculating WIF as introduced by Ingwersen (1998) i.e. the ratio of the number of links to a site, to the number of webpages at the site, has been used. This can be stated thus:

A = Total number of webpages to a particular site

B = Total Number of Internal links to a given site

C = Total Number of External links to a given site

D = Total number of links (External + Internal) to a site

Therefore, WIF (Simple) = **D/A**; WIF (Internal) = **B/A,** and WIF (External) = **C/A.**

In this study online SEO report generation tool, Neil Patel's SEO Analyzer (https://neilpatel.com/seo-analyzer/) has also been used to analyse and compare India's top most educational institutes of eminence websites on various parameters like page size, load time, SEO score and speed score. For finding out the Indian and global popularity ranking of the selected websites Alexa (https://www.alexa.com/siteinfo) tool has been used.

SCOPE OF THE STUDY

The websites of 18 academic institutes of eminence in India have been considered for this webometric analysis as 2 institutes e.g. Jio Institute (Reliance Foundation, Maharashtra) and Bharti (Satya Bharti Foundation, Delhi) websites are not yet in shape. The table 2.1 represents the brief details of those institutes with their websites' domain extensions.

Table 2.1. List of Selected Indian Institutes of Eminence

SL No	Name of the Institute	URL	Abbvr.	State	Year of Establishment	Domain Extn.
			Public			
1	IIT Madras	https://www.iitm.ac.in/	IIT Mad	Tamil Nadu	1959	.ac.in
2	IISc, Bengalore	https://www.iisc.ac.in/	IISc Bang	Karnataka	1909	.ac.in
3	IIT Delhi	http://www.iitd.ac.in/	IIT Delhi	Delhi	1961	.ac.in
4	IIT Bombay	http://www.iitb.ac.in/	IIT Bom	Maharashtra	1958	.ac.in
5	IIT Kharagpur	http://www.iitkgp.ac.in/	IIT Khag	West Bengal	1951	.ac.in
6	Benaras Hindu University	http://www.bhu.ac.in/	BHU	Uttar Pradesh	1916	.ac.in
7	University of Hyderabad	https://www.uohyd.ac.in/	UH	Telangana	1974	.ac.in
8	Jadavpur University	http://www.jaduniv.edu.in/	JU	West Bengal	1955	.edu.in
9	Anna University	https://www.annauniv.edu/	AU	Tamil Nadu	1978	.edu
10	Delhi University	http://du.ac.in/adm2019/	DU	Delhi	1922	.ac.in
			Private			
11	BITS Pilani,	https://www.bits-pilani.ac.in/	BITS	Rajasthan	1964	.ac.in
12	Manipal Academy of Higher Education	https://manipal.edu/mu.html	MAHE	Karnataka	1953	.edu
13	Amrita Vishwa Vidyapeetham, Bangalore	https://www.amrita.edu/	AVV	Karnataka	1994	.edu

14	VIT Vellore,Tami Nadu	https://vit.ac.in/	VITV	Tamil Nadu	1984	.ac.in
15	Jamia Hamdard, New Delhi	http://jamiahamdard.edu/	JH	Delhi	1989	.edu
16	Kalinga Instt. of Industrial Technology, Bhubaneswar	https://kiit.ac.in/	KIIT	Odisha	1999	.ac.in
17	O.P JINDAL University, Haryana	https://jgu.edu.in/	OPJU	Haryana	2009	.edu.in
18	Shiv Nadar University, Uttar Pradesh	https://www.snu.edu.in/	SNU	Uttar Pradesh	2011	.edu.in

Distribution of Domain Name Extensions

Domain name is a very important issue for any website. A domain suffix or 'top-level domain' (TLD) is intended to define the type of website and it impacts on webpage visibility and SEO score. From the above table (Table 2.1) and the following figure (Figure 2.1) it can be concluded that 61% websites have .ac.in domain extensions and remaining 22% websites have .edu and 17% websites have .edu.in domain extension.

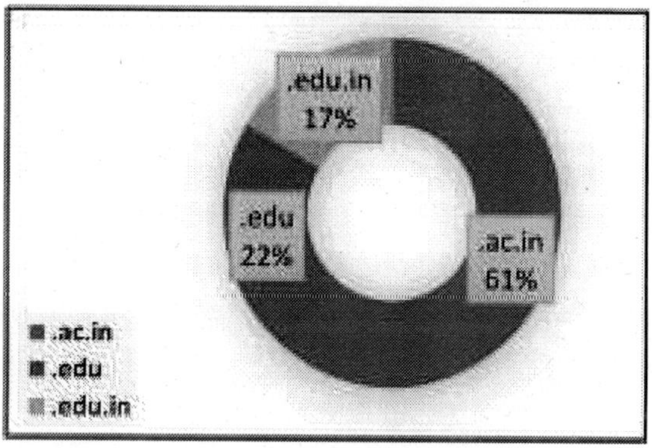

Fig. 2.1. Distribution of Domain Extensions

DATA ANALYSIS AND FINDINGS

Calculation of Web Impact Factors (WIF)

The following table illustrates three types of WIF distribution of the selected Indian academic institute websites with their webpage and link details. No link details have been found for the website of Kalinga Institute of Industrial Technology, Bhubaneswar.

Table 2.2. Web Impact Factors of Selected Websites

Name of the Academic Institute	*Number of Web Pages and Links*				*3 Types of Web Impact Factors*		
	Total No. of Webpage (A)	*Total No. of Inlinks (B)*	*Total No. of Extn. Links (C)*	*Total No. of Links (D)*	*Simple WIF (D/A)*	*Internal -link WIF (B/A)*	*External -link WIF (C/A)*
IIT Mad	92,000	43	62	105	0.001	0.0004	0.0006
IISc Bang	239,000	95	50	145	0.0006	0.0003	0.0002
IIT Delhi	803,000	95	51	146	0.0001	0.0001	0.00006
IIT Bom	436,000	103	37	140	0.0003	0.0002	0.00008
IIT Khag	63,000	120	86	206	0.003	0.0019	0.0013
BHU	23,200	194	20	204	0.008	0.0083	0.0008
UH	25,300	188	28	216	0.008	0.0074	0.0011
JU	11,400	147	24	171	0.015	0.0128	0.0021
AU	19,500	62	26	88	0.004	0.0031	0.0013
DU	120,000	212	13	225	0.001	0.0017	0.0001
BITS	19,200	87	18	105	0.005	0.0095	0.0009
MAHE	52,400	105	9	114	0.002	0.0020	0.0001
AVV	66,400	167	7	174	0.002	0.0025	0.00001
VITV	9,750	109	31	140	0.014	0.0111	0.0031
JH	1,300	152	52	204	0.156	0.1169	0.04
KIIT	12,300	-	-	-	-	-	-
OPJU	8,480	55	62	117	0.013	0.0064	0.0073
SNU	10,500	126	25	151	0.014	0.012	0.0023

Table 2.2 clearly denotes that according to the Simple Web Impact Factor (SWIF) ranking website of Jamia Hamdard (JH), New Delhi, holds the numerouno status with SWIF of 0.156. According to Internal –link Web Impact Factor (IWIF) and External-link Web Impact Factor (EWIF) the same institute holds the rank one position with 0.1169 and 0.04 respectively. Jadavpur University website holds the second spot according to SWIF (i.e. 0.015) and IWIF (i.e. 0.0128). Shiv Nadar University, Uttar Pradesh website has the second best EWIF of 0.0023.

Popularity Rank of Websites

Website popularity ranking is another important indicator which helps to better promotion of a website. Ranking of a website is based on a combined measure of page views and unique site users. Popularity ranking of selected Indian academic institute websites is portrayed through table 2.3. IIT Delhi website has the best Indian ranking i.e. 390 and Delhi University website has the best global ranking i.e. 3437.

Table 2.3. Popularity Ranking of the Websites

Institute	*Global Rank*	*Ranking in India*
IIT Mad	8,257	724
IISc Bang	29,278	2,636
IIT Delhi	8,140	390
IIT Bom	9,203	778
IIT Khag	9,313	857
BHU	35,440	3,702
UH	54,329	7,636
JU	54,368	7,427
AU	17,077	1,891
DU	3,437	397
BITS	26,402	1,918
MAHE	35,581	4,012
AVV	37,012	5,476
VITV	16,717	1,224
JH	202,478	31,988
KIIT	74,520	8,888
OPJU	279,574	29,336
SNU	109,812	9,930

Table 2.4. Page Size and Load Time of the Websites

Institute Name	*Page Size (MB/KB)*	*Load Time (Sec.)*
IIT Mad	509.7 KB	16.11
IISc Bang	924.6 KB	7.21
IIT Delhi	293.7 KB	0.47
IIT Bom	2.2 MB	63.53
IIT Khag	221.9 KB	30.09
BHU	1.1 MB	14.64
UH	1.0 MB	8.17
JU	1.4 MB	1.01
AU	204.6 KB	5.02
DU	1.4 MB	2.94
BITS	1.2 MB	4.44
MAHE	893.5 KB	16.97
AVV	70.2 KB	17.32
VITV	519.9 KB	1.96
JH	1.2 MB	26.73
KIIT	188.1 KB	13.04
OPJU	561.8 KB	9.08

Table 2.4 denotes that IIT Bombay has the heaviest webpage and i.e. 2.2 MB and consequently it has the worst load time of 63.53seconds. IIT Delhi website and Jadavpur University websites boast of little load time of 0.47 and 1.01 seconds consequently.

Results from SEO Analyzer

Web traffic is known as the collective number of visitors to a website. Search Engine Optimization increases the web traffic by making the website more visible to search engines (Sarkar, Pal &Kar, 2018). In the figure 2.2 the Traffic score, Speed Score and SEO Score of the websites have been depicted. O.P JINDAL University, Haryana website has the best SEO score and Traffic Score of 89 and 60 respectively. University of Hyderabad website has the best Speed Score of 84.

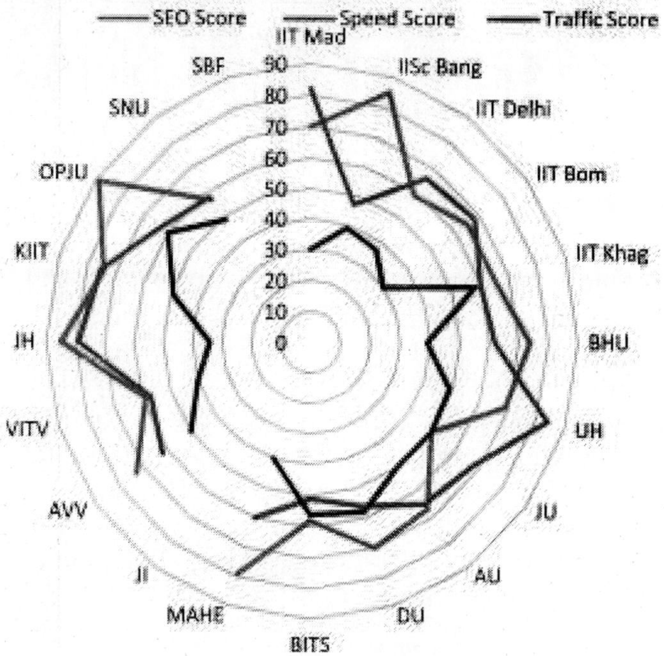

Fig. 2.2. SEO Analysis Scores

Domain and Page Authority

Page Authority (PA) is a score that predicts how well a specific page will rank on search engine result pages (SERP). Page Authority scores range from 1 to 100, with higher scores corresponding to a greater ability to rank. Whereas Page Authority measures the predictive ranking strength of a single page, Domain Authority measures the strength of entire domains or subdomains (MOZ, n.d.). Domain Authority (DA) is a search engine ranking score that predicts how well a website will rank on search engine result pages (SERPs). A Domain Authority score ranges from 1 to 100, with higher scores corresponding to a greater ability to rank (MOZ, n.d.).These were developed by MOZ, a software as a service (SaaS) company based in USA.

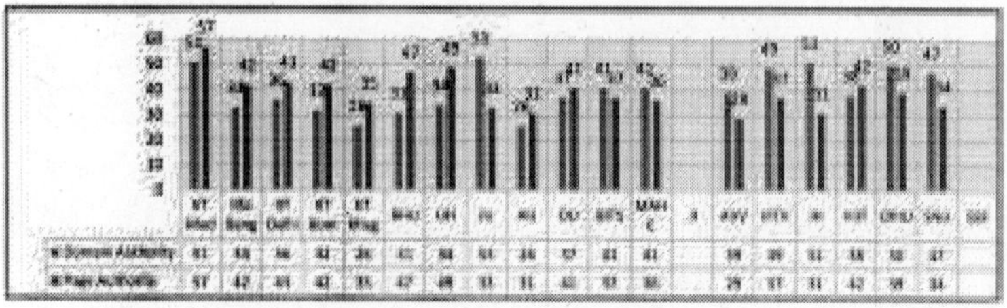

Fig. 2.3. Distribution of Domain and Page Authority

Figure 2.3 depicts that Jadavpur University website has the highest domain authority score of 53 and IIT Kharagpur and Anna University both have the least (26) domain authority score. On the other hand IIT Madras has the highest page authority score of 57 and Amrita VishwaVidyapeetham, Bangalore has the least page authority score of 29. IIT Madras with second highest domain authority score (51) and page authority score signifies the website's good rank on search engine result pages.

Link Topology of the Websites

World popular web crawler SocSciBot (http://socscibot.wlv.ac.uk/) was used to collect the required data from the India's Institutes of Eminence websites. The crawler provides some analytical tools and returns the data in a form which can be easily imported in common network analysis programs. For Social Network Analysis (SAN) and visualization, the Pajek software has been used. Pajek allows better diagrams than illustrated in the instructions - including coloured nodes and variable width nodes and arcs. The network diagram (figure 2.4) showing links among the websites covered in this study is given bellow.

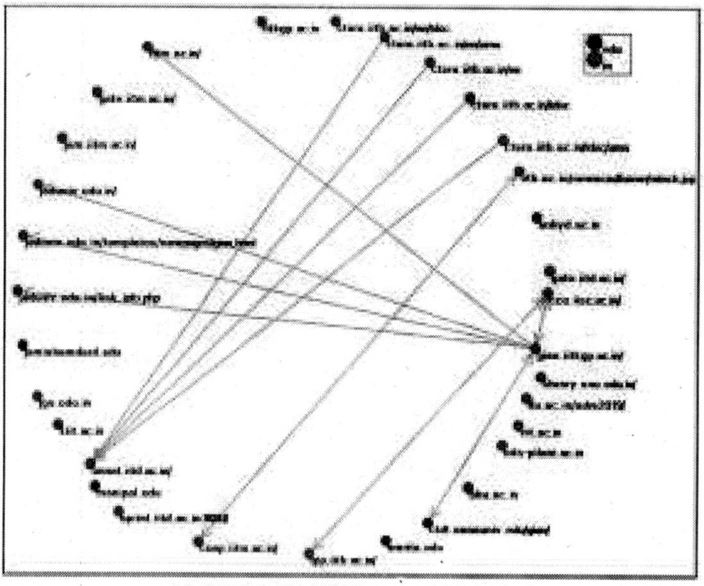

Fig. 2.4. Mapping the Links of Institutes of Eminence in India (Pajek)

CONCLUSIONS

This quantitative analysis of the websites of 18 Institutes of Eminence upholds some of the qualities of these websites. While according to Simple Web Impact Factor (SWIF), Internal-link Web Impact Factor (IWIF) and External- link Web Impact Factor (EWIF) ranking website of Jamia Hamdard (JH), New Delhi, holds the numerouno status. IIT Delhi website has the best Indian ranking i.e. 390 and Delhi University website has the best global ranking i.e. 3437. IIT Bombay has the heaviest webpage and i.e. 2.2 MB and consequently it has the worst load time of 63.53seconds. IIT Delhi website and Jadavpur University websites boast of little load time of 0.47 and 1.01 seconds consequently. Jadavpur University website has the highest domain authority score of 53 and IIT Madras has the highest page authority score of 57.

REFERENCES

- *Alexa.* (n.d.). Retrieved September 10, 2019, from https://www.alexa.com/siteinfo
- Babu, B.R., Jeyshankar, R., & Nageswara Rao, P. (2013). Websites of Central Universities in India: A webometric analysis. *DESIDOC Journal of Library and Information Technology, 30*(2), 33-43.
- Ingwersen, P. (1998). The calculation of web impact factors. *Journal of Documentation, 54*(2), 236-43.
- Jakopec, T., Hoare, C., & Riordan, R. O. (2012). Web connectivity of higher education institutions within a country: A comparison of Croatia and Ireland. In *Proceedings of the ITI 2012, 34th International Conference on Information Technology Interfaces*, June 25-28.
- Jalal, S. K., Biswas, S. C., &Mukhopadhyay, P. (2010). Web impact factor and link analysis of selected Indian Universities. *Annals of Library and Information Studies,* 57(June), 109-121.
- MOZ. (n.d.). *Domain authority.* Retrieved from https://moz.com/learn/seo/domain-authority.
- MOZ. (n.d.). *Page authority.* Retrieved from https://moz.com/learn/seo/page-authority.
- MOZ. (n.d.). *Meta description.* Retrieved from https://moz.com/learn/seo/meta-description.
- Noruzi, A. (2005). Web impact factors for Iranian universities. *Webology, 2*(1). Retrieved September 14, 2019, from http://www.webology.ir/2005/v2n1/a11.html
- Patel, N. (n.d.). *SEO analyzer.* Retrieved September 13, 2019, from https://neilpatel.com/seo-analyzer/
- Press Information Bureau, Government of India (2019). 20 institutions recommended for status of 'Institutions of Eminence'. Retrieved from https://pib.gov.in/newsite/PrintRelease.aspx?relid=192458
- Sarkar, A. & Pal, A. (2018). Websites of Indian banks: A webomeric study. *Library Philosophy and Practice (e-journal),* 2209, 1-18.
- Sarkar, A., Pal, A., & Kar, S. (2018). Webometric mapping of tourism sites in India. *Library Philosophy and Practice (e-journal), 1957,* 1-14.

3

Webometric Mapping of Indian Tourism Sites

ABSTRACT

Website is the mirror of an organization or institution. This webometrics study is performed on the government tourism websites in India. The present paper highlights the global SEO ranking with various scores and popularity ranking of the tourism websites in India. Traffic score, speed score, page size and load time of the websites have been reflected in this study to reveal the quality of the websites. Collecting data using SocSciBot 4 web crawler and designing a network topology using Pajek network design software have added much to its panoramic visualization.

Keywords: Tourism in India, Webometrics, Search Engine Optimization, Web Crawler

INTRODUCTION

Information and communication technologies (ICT) have had a remarkable impact on the tourism sector in the 21st century. In recent years, a considerable number of experts have shown interest in the significance of innovations in tourism sector and have analyzed the impact of ICT to tourism services and their competitiveness. The fast growing tourism industry of India is highly important from economic perspective. The World Travel & Tourism Council calculated that tourism generated a good percentage of the nation's GDP. The Ministry of Tourism functions as the nodal agency for the development of tourism in the country. It plays a vital role in coordinating and supplementing the efforts of the State/Union Territory governments. Tourism business is promoted by the State/Union Territory governments through their individual websites which offer a wide range of tour and travel related information, with their wide range of activities, as compared to other types of industrial, cultural and those types of websites. The present paper attempts to analyse and evaluate India's tourism websites on the basis of Search Engine Optimization (SEO) rank and Alexa page-ranking. Mapping of the links using SocSciBot and Pajek software is also the forte of this paper.

TOURISM IN INDIA

India, the land of mystery and nature's sublime beauty had its magical charm on the tourists from different corners of the world since antiquity. Observing her inextricable appeal to the foreigners, tourism business in India flourished by leaps and bounds. With this in mind Indian government opened a separate sector in the name of Ministry of Tourism in 1967. In 2016 this sector earned a hefty sum of 208.9 billion US dollar and with a budget of 330million US dollar for the financial year 2018-19, India's tourism business only hinted at its blooming status. India has also jumped 12 places to 40th rank globally in the travel and tourism competitiveness list by World Economic Forum (WEF) according to Travel& Tourism Competitiveness Report 2017 (WEF, 2018). Tourism in its different colours like religious and spiritual tourism, medical tourism, adventure tourism, cultural tourism, ecotourism, heritage tourism and domestic tourism is flagrant in India where not only the foreigners but the Indian travelers also loiter from Kashmir to Kanyakumari only to drink deep into the panoramic euphoria of the land of seven rivers. Many studies (Thanh-Dam, 1983; Rao, 1999; Sreekumar, 2002; Bandyopadhyay, 2013) have pointed out that India is a centre of sex tourism. The Centre for Agriculture and Bioscience International (CABI) says that India is a haven for sex tourism. Goa is the most preferred place to the foreigners followed by Mumbai, Delhi and Kerala for liberal attitude and gorgeous beaches. Rao (1997) discussed issues on women and tourism in Kerala, including consideration of tourism as a part of modern consumerism and the sex industry. Paul, L. (2003) said that unfortunately children are also involved with this nasty profession. Govt. of India is trying to resolve the problems by adopting laws, regulations and spreading awareness. The figure 3.1 and table 3.2 indicate the remarkable growing trend of tourists' attraction towards India.

Table 3.1. Foreign Exchange Earnings (FEEs) through Tourism (in Rs. terms)

Year	*Earnings (Crores)*	*% change*
2001	15,083	"3.5
2002	15,064	"0.1
2003	20,729	37.6
2004	27,944	34.8
2005	33,123	18.5
2006	39,025	17.8
2007	44,360	13.7
2008	51,294	15.6
2009	53,700	4.7
2010	64,889	20.8
2011	77,591	19.6
2012	94,487	21.8

2013	1,07,671	14
2014	1,23,320	14.5
2015	1,35,193	8.8
2016	1,54,146	14
2017	1,80,379	17

Source: Sanjay Kumar "Foreign Exchange Earnings through Tourism in India in December 2017".

The above table (Table 3.1) clearly reflects that Foreign Exchange Earnings (FEEs) have been increasing profusely with every passing year which only hints at the lucrative tourism business in India.

Fig. 3.1. Arrival of Foreign Tourists in India (including nationals of Pakistan and Bangladesh)

Data Source: IndiaStat.Com (Lok Sabha Starred Question No. 130, dated on 05.03.2018 & Lok Sabha Question No. 235, dated on 02.03.2018, Ministry of Tourism, Govt. of India. (ON1647) Past Issues.)

Table 3.2. Foreign and Domestic Tourist Visitors in 2015

Rank	*State/Union*	*Number*	*Share (%)*
	Share of top 10 states/UTs of India in number of foreign tourist visits in 2015		
1	Tamil Nadu	4684707	20
2	Maharashtra	4408916	19
3	Uttar Pradesh	3104062	13
4	Delhi	2379169	10
5	Rajasthan	1489500	6.4
6	West Bengal	1475311	6.3
7	Kerala	977479	4.2
8	Bihar	923737	4
9	Karnataka	636502	2.7
10	Goa	541480	2.3
	Top 10 states	**20620863**	**88**
	Other	**2705300**	**12**
	Total	**23326163**	**100**
	Share of top 10 states/UTs of India in number of domestic tourist visits in 2015		
1	Tamil Nadu	333459047	23.3
2	Uttar Pradesh	204888457	14.3
3	Andhra Pradesh	121591054	8.5
4	Karnataka	119863942	8.4
5	Maharashtra	103403934	7.2
6	Telangana	94516316	6.6
7	Madhya Pradesh	77975738	5.4
8	West Bengal	70193450	4.9
9	Gujrat	36288463	2.5
10	Rajasthan	35187573	2.5
	Top 10 states	**1197367974**	**83.6**
	Other	**234605820**	**16.4**
	Total	**1431973794**	**100**

Source: India Tourism Statistics at a Glance 2017

The table 3.2 clearly hints at the dominance of Tamilnadu in receiving foreign and domestic tourists in the year 2015. Maharashtra and Uttarpradesh are not very far behind in the list.

LITERATURE REVIEW

Kumar, K. (2017) conducted a webometrics study on the websites of deemed universities in Andhra Pradesh and Telangana and analyzed the web impact factor. He had examined 7 deemed university websites and identified number of web pages and link pages, and calculated Web Impact Factor (WIF) using Google search engine. The websites were ranked based on these Webometric indicators. The study revealed that websites of Andhra Pradesh's universities have more number of web-pages but the websites of Telangana's universities have high web impact factor in most of the parameters.

Biswas, Pal & Kar (2018) in their study emphasized on the websites of the 12 Government Medical College and Hospitals of West Bengal. After analysing the various types of links of the said websites, Web Impact Factor (WIF) of different types had been calculated and on the basis of WIFs three types of ranking of the websites had been delineated. The paper established the supremacy of the North Bengal Medical College and Hospital website in all the three WIF lists.

Zeinolabedini, Maktabifard and Osareh (2006) studied that various national libraries' status depend on their website's quality and performance. Results of this research showed that Library of Congress website is the most powerful one among the world's other national library websites.

OBJECTIVES OF THE STUDY

The objectives of the present study are as follows:

- To find out the visibility and performance of Indian tourism websites.

- To calculate the domain extension percentage of the websites.
- To examine the link-quality of selected tourism websites in India.
- To analyse and evaluate the tourism websites of India on the basis of SEO.
- To find out the global popularity ranking of the websites.

SCOPE AND COVERAGE

In India, there are 29 states and 7 union territories that create a federal constitutional republic structure under a parliamentary system. Only Government tourism sites have been considered for the present study. All the 36 websites have been considered for the present study. The study is restricted within the particular time period i.e. from 15/07/2018 to 30/07/2018. Tourism related blogs and other sites have been kept outside the purview of the study in spite of their enormous amount of information for the tourists.

METHODOLOGY

Tourism websites have been taken from the official website of Ministry of Tourism, Govt. of India and different search engines. All the selected websites are analysed with the help of online tools like Neil Patel's SEO analyser (https://neilpatel.com/seo-analyzer/) and Alexa (https://www.alexa.com/siteinfo). After the of data collection, the collected data were analysed and tabulated keeping in view the objectives of the study. SocSciBot (http://socscibot.wlv.ac.uk/) and Pajek software were also used to visualize the network mapping of the websites.

RESULTS AND DISCUSSION

Domain name is a very important issue for any website. A domain suffix or top-level domain (TLD) is intended to define the type of website and it impacts on webpage visibility and SEO score. In this figure 3.2, 36 Indian tourism websites were grouped under six domain extensions as reflected in their URLs. Most of the websites have .gov.in (58.33%) extension, followed by.com (16.67%), .org (11.11), .nic.in (8.33%), .in (2.78%) and.html (2.78%).

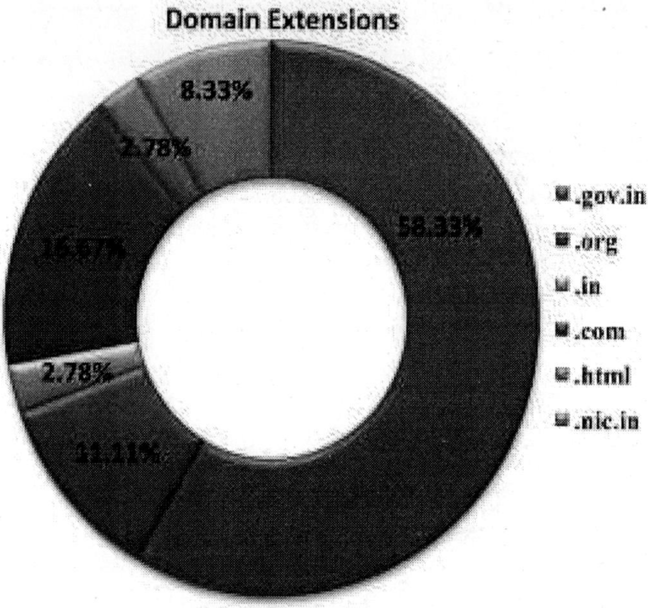

Fig. 3.2. Domain Extension Percentages

VISIBILITY AND WEB-TRAFFIC

Web traffic is known as the collective number of visitors to a website. Search Engine Optimization increases the web traffic by making the website more visible to search engines. In this study online SEO report generation tool, Neil Patel's SEO analyser (https://neilpatel.com/seo-analyzer/) has been used to analyse and compare India's state and union territory tourism websites on various parameters like backlinks, page size, load time, request, traffic score, SEO score and speed score.

Table-3.3 shows the number of backlinks, page size, load time and request of 36 tourism websites. With the

Table 3.3. Results from SEO Analyzer

	Name of states	*URL*	*Back links*	*Page size (KB/MB)*	*Loadtime (Sec.)*	*Request*
1	Andaman & Nicobar	http://www.andamans.gov.in	147	1.5MB	4.11	50
2	Andhra Pradesh	http://www.aptourism.gov.in	50	1.0MB	4.96	40
3	Arunachal Pradesh	http://www.arunachaltourism.com/#0	212	1.0MB	1.71	46
4	Assam	http://www.assamtourismonline.com/	38	643.8KB	0.78	43
5	Bihar	http://bstdc.bih.nic.in/	5184	3.4MB	9.32	86
6	Chandigarh	http://chandigarhtourism.gov.in	150	98.6KB	3.35	15
7	Chhattisgarh	http://cgtourism.choice.gov.in/	8	10.0MB	7.62	176
8	Dadra-Nagar Haveli	http://dnh.nic.in/Tourism/destinations.html	453	161.8KB	2.79	45
9	Daman and Diu	http://www.daman.nic.in/	805	2.5 MB	12.01	84
10	Goa	http://www.goatourism.gov.in	289	551.2KB	12.64	43
11	Gujarat	http://www.gujarattourism.com/	711	1.2MB	56.57	54
12	Haryana	http://haryanatourism.gov.in	224	2.5MB	6.04	128
13	Himachal Pradesh	http://hptdc.nic.in	75	6.7MB	8.61	188
14	Jammu & Kashmir	http://www.jktourism.org/	333	8.6MB	23.27	245
15	Jharkhand	http://jharkhandtourism.gov.in/	25	5.0MB	32.39	232
16	Karnataka	http://www.karnatakatourism.org/	295	1.3MB	16.12	104
17	Kerala	http://www.keralatourism.org	905	2.2MB	8.77	110
18	Lakshadweep	http://lakshadweeptourism.com/	104	139.6KB	0.82	24
19	Madhya Pradesh	http://www.mptourism.com	570	3.7MB	5.52	114

20	Maharashtra	http://www.maharashtratourism.gov.in/	530	2.6MB	4.80	57
21	Manipur	http://www.manipurtourism.gov.in/	34	3.3MB	8.56	155
22	Meghalaya	http://megtourism.gov.in	204	1.2MB	5.53	47
23	Mizoram	https://tourism.mizoram.gov.in	207	1.4MB	5.45	53
24	Nagaland	http://tourismnagaland.com/	112	1.3MB	6.00	67
25	New Delhi	http://www.delhitourism.gov.in/delhit ourism/ index.jsp	585	894.6KB	7.74	69
26	Odisha	http://www.odishatourism.gov.in	145	1.7MB	16.53	111
27	Puducherry	http://tourism.puducherry.gov.in/	1670	588.8KB	4.57	45
28	Punjab	http://www.punjabtourism.gov.in	116	4.3MB	7.57	128
29	Rajasthan	http://www.tourism.rajasthan.gov.in/	6108	2.7MB	6.19	126
30	Sikkim	http://www.sikkimtourism.gov.in/	167	838.0KB	5.36	47
31	Tamil Nadu	http://www.tamilnadutourism.org	681	3.7MB	5.13	63
32	Telangana	http://www.telanganatourism.gov.in/	281	6.6MB	16.96	152
33	Tripura	http://tripuratourism.gov.in	91	1.7MB	44.09	120
34	Uttar Pradesh	http://www.uptourism.gov.in	188	5.6MB	11.48	221
35	Uttarakhand	http://uttarakhandtourism.gov.in/	194	7.4MB	16.74	265
36	West Bengal	http://www.wbtourism.gov.in	34	2.9MB	7.60	109

good amount of quality backlinks, one can not only attract a remarkable number of visitors to their website but also can improve their website's ranking. Rajasthan (6108) has highest number of backlinks and then followed by websites of Bihar (5184), Puducherry (1670), Kerala (905), Daman-Diu (805) and Gujarat (711). Page size of a website, the indicatorof the amount of data to be spent to load the site, is a very important parameter of SEO. In this regard, Chhattisgarh (10.0 MB) has topped the list. After the website of Chhattisgarh websites of Jammu & Kashmir (8.6 MB), Uttarakhand (7.4 MB), Himachal Pradesh (6.7 MB) and Telangana (6.6 MB) maintain their order. Website load time is another important indicator of SEO. Users' satisfactions or dissatisfactions are very much dependent on website loading time. Above table shows that website of Assam is the fastest loading website with 0.78 seconds and then followed by websites of Lakshadweep (0.82 sec.), Arunachal Pradesh (1.71 sec.), Dadra-Nagar Haveli (2.79 sec.) and Chandigarh (3.35 sec.). In case of request website of Uttarakhand (265) has topped the list, followed by Jammu & Kashmir (245), Jharkhand (232), Uttar Pradesh (221) and Himachal Pradesh (188). Based on these above four parameters, following scores are given by Neil Patel's SEO analyser that is distributed through figure-3.3 and table-3.4 (See Appendix-1).

It is evident from the table-3.4 and figure 3.3 that no single website tops all three categories of ranking. Whereas website of Rajasthan (74) receives highest traffic and is followed by websites of Bihar (66), Puducherry (57), Kerala (52), Gujarat (50) and New Delhi (50). In the list of SEO score Mizoram holds the numero uno status with a score of 85 while websites of Andhra Pradesh, Dadra-Nagar Haveli, Goa and Gujarat (each having SEO score of 84) have done well and those are followed by Jharkhand (83) and Meghalaya (83), Andaman Nicobar (82) and Himachal Pradesh (82), Bihar (81) and Maharashtra (80). Tourism website of Goa (77) has topped the speed score and is followed by Andhra Pradesh (75) and Lakshadweep (72).

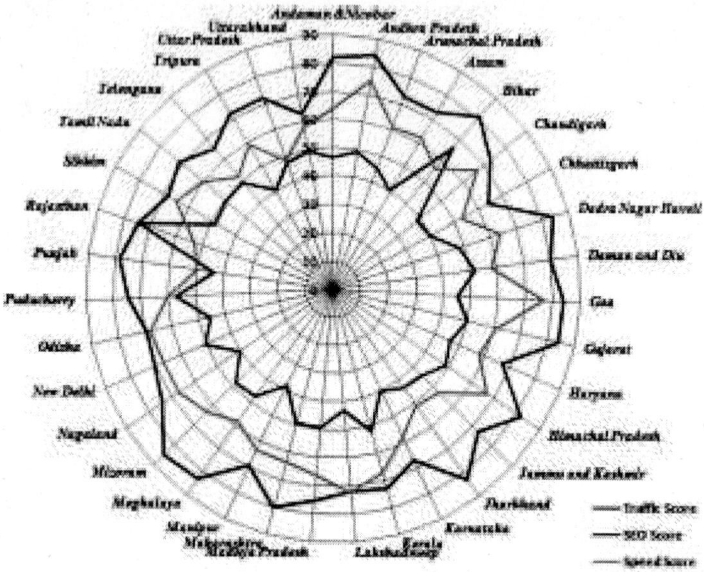

Fig. 3.3. Traffic Score, SEO Score, Speed Score

POPULARITY RANK OF WEBSITES

Website popularity ranking is another important indicator which helps to better promotion of a website. Ranking of a website is based on a combined measure of page views and unique site users. Popularity ranking of selected state and union territory tourism websites is described below through the following table 3.5.

Table 3.5 reflects that, according to popularity test, tourism website of Rajasthan (705 and 712) is the most popular website by Neil Patel's SEO analyser and Alexa. After the website of Rajasthan most popular websites are Bihar (5102 and 5071), Puducherry (48835 and 48886), Mizoram (81595 and 81522) and Kerala (95519 and 95658). This table also shows that there is very little difference between two ranks provided by Neil Patel's SEO analyser and Alexa.

Table 3.5. Popularity Rank of the Websites

	Name of NL Website	URL	Rank by Neilpatel.com	Alexa page rank
1	Andaman & Nicobar	http://www.andamans.gov.in	540 659	542 084
2	Andhra Pradesh	http://www.aptourism.gov.in	297 883	295 770
3	Arunachal Pradesh	http://www.arunachaltourism.com/#0	634 733	632 548
4	Assam	http://www.assamtourismonline.com/	1 016 708	999 550
5	Bihar	http://bstdc.bih.nic.in/	510 2	507 1
6	Chandigarh	http://chandigarhtourism.gov.in	2 055 693	2 010 428
7	Chhattisgarh	http://cgtourism.choice.gov.in/	1 538 149	1 639 904
8	Dadra - Nagar Haveli	http://dnh.nic.in/Tourism/destinations.html	349 868	348 388
9	Daman and Diu	http://www.daman.nic.in/	94,075	93,034
10	Goa	http://www.goatourism.gov.in	693 987	688 678
11	Gujarat	http://www.gujarattourism.com/	180 308	179 652
12	Haryana	http://haryanatourism.gov.in	590 591	588 353
13	Himachal Pradesh	http://hptdc.nic in	215 888	350 301
14	Jammu and Kashmir	http://www.jktourism.org/	736 325	740 561
15	Jharkhand	http://jharkhandtourism.gov.in/	815 177	815 155
16	Karnataka	http://www.karnatakatourism.org/	1019811	1019811
17	Kerala	http://www.keralatourism.org	95 519	95 658
18	Lakshadweep	http://lakshadweeptourism.com/	870 573	889 273
19	Madhya Pradesh	http://www.mptourism.com	220 226	221 548

20	Maharashtra	http://www.maharashtratourism.gov.in/	208 462	209 608
21	Manipur	http://www.manipurtourism.gov.in/	3 172 761	3 301 065
22	Meghalaya	http://megtourism.gov.in	463 313	454 426
23	Mizoram	https://tourism.mizoram.gov.in	81 595	81 522
24	Nagaland	http://tourismnagaland.com/	1 518 009	1 518 184
25	New Delhi	http://www.delhitourism.gov.in/delhitourism/index.jsp	157 317	157 255
26	Odisha	http://www.odishatourism.gov.in	632 391	632 359
27	Puducherry	http://tourism.puducherry.gov.in/	48 835	48 886
28	Punjab	http://www.punjabtourism.gov.in	811 890	801 902
29	Rajasthan	http://www.tourism.rajasthan.gov.in/	705	712
30	Sikkim	http://www.sikkimtourism.gov.in/	387 186	382 963
31	Tamil Nadu	http://www.tamilnadutourism.org	212 374	212 001
32	Tripura	http://tripuratourism.gov.in	1 100 253	1 102 212
33	Telengana	http://www.telanganatourism.gov.in/	248 071	248 071
34	Uttar Pradesh	http://www.uptourism.gov.in	405 924	405 124
35	Uttarakhand	http://uttarakhandtourism.gov.in/	261 522	263 808
36	West Bengal	http://www.wbtourism.gov.in	573 570	568 637

LINK MAPPING OF SITES

World popular web crawler SocSciBot (http://socscibot.wlv.ac.uk/) was used to collect the required data (Christopoulos, 2014) from the India's tourism web sites. The crawler provides some analytical tools and returns the data in a form which can be easily imported in common network analysis programs. The web harvesting was conducted on 25.07.2018-27.07.2018. For Social Network Analysis (SAN) and visualization, the Pajek (De Nooy, 2018) software was used. Pajek allows better diagrams than illustrated in the instructions - including coloured nodes and variable width nodes and arcs. The network diagram showing links between 36 tourism sites covered in this study is given bellow. The figure-3.4 shows that, Delhi tourism site (delhitourism.gov.in) is linked with maximum tourism sites of India. Delhi tourism site is linked with Maharashtra, Goa, Taminnadu, Rajasthan, Andaman, Gujrat, Chandigarh, Haryana, Bihar and other tourism sites. Haryana tourism site is also linked with Punjab and Jharkhand tourism sites. The states of North East India, Arunachal Pradesh, Meghalay, Nagaland, Tripura, Sikim, Monipur, Assam, Mizoram are connected with each other. So there is a collaborative venture among the states of North East India that leads tourists to discover the natural beauty of eastern India.

CONCLUSION

All the government tourism sites of India are well designed and structured and maximum websites are hosted by NIC. All the sites have visualized their local festivals, food habits, historical, cultural, geographical information and heritage of the particular State/Union Territory. A few websites are linked with each other. SEO Analyser shows, Rajasthan (6108) has highest number of backlinks and Chhattisgarh has lowest (8) number of backlinks. It is expected that all the tourism sites have large number of images related to site views and other

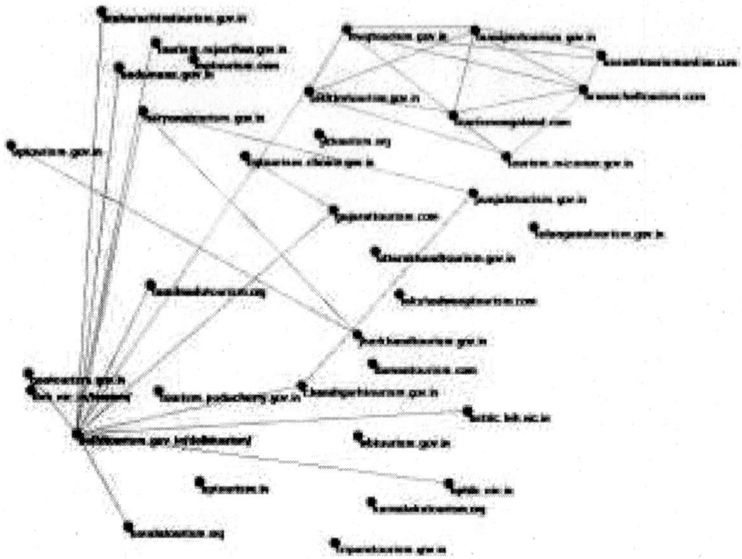

Fig. 3.4. Mapping of India Tourism Sites (Pajek)

information. So, the page size gets increased likewise. But speed factor is also an issue for a good website. Chhattisgarh has the largest page size with 10 MB with a loading time of 7.62 sec. Dadra-Nagar Haveli (161.8KB) has lowest page size with a loading time of 2.79 sec. Users' satisfactions or dissatisfactions are very much dependent on website's loading time. Assam with a loading time of 0.78 sec and Gujrat with a loading time of 56.57 sec. stand in stark contrast to each other. This maximum loading time is a cause for dissatisfaction to an eager viewer. Chhattisgarh, Jharkhand, Manipur, West Bengal, Assam, Andhra Pradesh, Tripura and Lakshadweep need to improve backlinks number. North East India is growing in popularity as a tourist destination for its natural beauty in spite of its communication and other infrastructural problems. With the presence of links to App and social sites (like WhatsApp, Facebook, Twitter etc.),virtual reference service (like FAQ), logistics management and security related information only add much to the value of a tourism website. Webometrics study of tourism sites in India is an unexplored area of webometric research. These findings open the door to further studies of other new areas of the web and for longitudinal studies to chart the changing nature of the way in which communities use the Internet.

REFERENCES

- Ahmad Bakeri, A. B., & NurLeyni, N. P. J. (2015). Webometric study of world class universities websites. *Qualitative and Quantitative Methods in Libraries (QQML), Special Issue Bibliometrics and Scientometrics,* 105-115, Retrieved July 15, 2018, from www.qqml.net/.../4S11QQML_Journal_2015_SpecialIssueBibliometrics_AbuBakarBa
- Asnani, R. (2013). A webometric analysis of institutional repositories using Dspace in India. *INFLIBNET,* 20(4), 22-27, Retrieved from http://ir.inflibnet.ac.in:8080/ir/ViewerJS/#../bitstream/1944/1942/1/INFLIBNET%20Newsle tter.Vol.%2020-%20No.4%20 (October-December,%202013).pdf
- Bandyopadhyay, R. (2013). A paradigm shift in sex tourism research. *Tourism Management Perspectives, 6,* 1-2.
- Biswas, S., Pal, A., & Kar, S. (2018). A webometric analysis of government medical college and hospitals in West Bengal, *Granthagar, 68*(4), 7-13.
- Business maps of India. (n.d.). Retrieved July 28, 2018, from https://business.mapsofindia.com/
- CABI. (n.d.). India a haven for sex tourism. Leisure Tourism. Retrieved July 27, 2018 from https://www.cabi.org/leisuretourism/news/15135
- Christopoulos, D., & Aubke, F. (2014). Data collection for social network analysis in tourism research. *Knowledge Networks and Tourism,* 126-42.
- De Nooy, W., Mrvar, A., & Batagelj, V. (2018). *Exploratory social network analysis with Pajek.* New York: Cambridge University Press.
- *Heritage tourism.* (n.d.). Retrieved July 28, 2018, from https://en.wikipedia.org/wiki/Heritage_tourism
- Indiastat. (n.d.) Retrieved July 29, 2018, from https://

www.indiastat.com/table/tourism-data/29/foreign-tourists/280/1949/data.aspx

- *India tourism statistics at a glance 2017.* (2017). Retrieved July 28, 2018 from http://tourism.gov.in/sites/default/files/Other/english%20India%20Torurism%20Statics%20020917.pdf
- Kumar, K. (2017). Web impact factor analysis for deemed universities in Andhra Pradesh. *DESIDOC Journal of Library & Information Technology, 37*(2), 98-103, Retrieved from publications.drdo.gov.in/ojs/index.php/djlit/article/download/9992/5837
- Paul, L. (2003). Child sex tourism. *Tourism Recreation Research, 28*(2), 83-87,DOI: 10.1080/02508281.2003.11081407
- Rao, N. (1999). Sex tourism in south Asia. *International Journal of Contemporary Hospitality Management, 11*(2/3), 96-99.
- Rao, N. (1997). Women and tourism in Kerala. *ANLetter, 5*(3), 31-33.
- Sanjay Kumar (17 January 2018)."Foreign Exchange Earnings (in Rupee and US $ Terms) through Tourism in India in December 2017". Press Information Bureau, Government of India, Ministry of Tourism. Retrieved July 26, 2018 from http://pib.nic.in/newsite/PrintRelease.aspx?relid=175688
- Seth P. N. (1993). *Introduction to travel and tourism,* New Delhi: Sterling Publishers.
- Smith, M., Macleod, N. & Robertson, M. H. (2010). *Key concepts in tourist studies.* London: SAGE.
- Sreekumar, T. T., & Parayil, G. (2002). Contentions and contradictions of tourism as development option: the case of Kerala, India. *Third World Quarterly, 23*(3), 529-548.
- Thanh-Dam, T. (1983). The dynamics of sex tourism: The case of South-east Asia. *Development and Change, 14*(4), 533-553.
- Thanuskodi, S. (2012). A webometric analysis of selected institutes of national importance websites in India, *International Journal of Library Science, 1*(1), 13-18, Retrieved from article.sapub.org/pdf/10.5923.j.library.20120101.03.pdf

- *Tourism in India.* (n.d.). Retrieved July 28, 2018, from https://en.wikipedia.org/wiki/Tourism_in_India
- UK Essays. (2013). *A history of Indian tourism.* Retrieved from https://www.ukessays.com/essays/tourism/history-of-indian-tourism-tourism- essay. php?vref=1
- UNWTO, World Tourism Organization. (n.d.). Retrieved July 26, 2018, from http://www2.unwto.org/content/about-us-5
- World Economic Forum. (n.d.). Retrieved July 29, 2018, from http://reports.weforum.org/travel-and-tourism-competitiveness-report- 2017/ranking/?doing_wp_cron=1532833634.9339320659637451171875
- Zeinolabedinio, M. H., Maktabifard, L., & Osareh, F. (2006). Collaboration analysis of world national library websites via webometric methods. *E-prints in Library and Information Science,* Retrieved from http://eprints.rclis.org/7439/

APPENDIX 1

Table 3.4. Scores via SEO Analyzer

	Websites	*URL*	*Traffic Score*	*SEO Score*	*Speed Score*
1	Andaman &Nicobar	http://www.andamans.gov.in	46	82	64
2	Andhra Pradesh	http://www.aptourism.gov.in	49	84	75
3	Arunachal Pradesh	http://www.arunachaltourism.com/#0	45	73	61
4	Assam	http://www.assamtourismonline.com/	40	73	62
5	Bihar	http://bstdc.bih.nic.in/	66	81	56
6	Chandigarh	http://chandigarhtourism.gov.in	39	73	67
7	Chhattisgarh	http://cgtourism.choice.gov.in/	40	64	53
8	Dadra Nagar Haveli	http://dnh.nic.in/Tourism/destinations.html	48	84	64
9	Daman and Diu	http://www.daman.nic.in/	52	80	58
10	Goa	http://www.goatourism.gov.in	45	84	77
11	Gujarat	http://www.gujarattourism.com/	50	84	61
12	Haryana	http://haryanatourism.gov.in	46	67	58
13	Himachal Pradesh	http://hptdc.nic.in	49	82	67
14	Jammu and Kashmir	http://www.jktourism.org/	44	73	53
15	Jharkhand	http://jharkhandtourism.gov.in/	43	83	51
16	Karnataka	http://www.karnatakatourism.org/	40	67	58
17	Kerala	http://www.keralatourism.org	52	73	67
18	Lakshadweep	http://lakshadweeptourism.com/	43	72	72

19	Madhya Pradesh	http://www.mptourism.com	49	75	66
20	Maharashtra	http://www.maharashtratourism.gov.in/	49	80	63
21	Manipur	http://www.manipurtourism.gov.in/	38	69	63
22	Meghalaya	http://megtourism.gov.in	47	83	58
23	Mizoram	https://tourism.mizoram.gov.in	48	85	63
24	Nagaland	http://tourismnagaland.com/	40	74	67
25	New Delhi	http://www.delhitourism.gov.in/ delhitourism/index.jsp	50	70	67
26	Odisha	http://www.odishatourism.gov.in	45	69	68
27	Puducherry	http://tourism.puducherry.gov.in/	57	74	60
28	Punjab	http://www.punjabtourism.gov.in	43	78	50
29	Rajasthan	http://www.tourism.rajasthan.gov.in/	74	74	53
30	Sikkim	http://www.sikkimtourism.gov.in/	48	68	65
31	Tamil Nadu	http://www.tamilnadutourism.org	49	71	60
32	Telengana	http://www.telanganatourism.gov.in/	49	65	52
33	Tripura	http://tripuratourism.gov.in	40	72	59
34	Uttar Pradesh	http://www.uptourism.gov.in	47	72	48
35	Uttarakhand	http://uttarakhandtourism.gov.in/	49	63	58
36	West Bengal	http://www.wbtourism.gov.in	46	62	53

4

Websites of Indian Political Parties From Webometric Viewpoint

ABSTRACT

Web Impact Factor (WIF), Search Engine Optimization (SEO) etc. improve the visibility of a website's presence in online environment. The present study predominantly focuses on the WIFs of the Indian political party websites. Political parties in India are trying hard to impress the common mass through their websites. This quantitative analysis of the party websites upholds some of the qualities of these websites. While according to Simple Web Impact Factor (SWIF) and Internal-link Web Impact Factor (IWIF) ranking Telugu Desam Party (TDP) holds the numero uno status, in case of External-link Web Impact Factor (EWIF), YSR Congress Party holds the rank one position. Lok Janshakti Party website has the maximum loading time (32.21 seconds) whereas AamAadmi Party website is the fastest to load its page in only 0.64 seconds. *Lok Janshakti*

Party website has the maximum traffic score of 60. Nationalist Congress Party and *Rashtriya Janata Dal* both have the maximum SEO score of 89. Nationalist Congress Party again tops the list with maximum speed score of 85.

Keywords : Web Impact Factor, WIF, Search Engine Optimization, SEO, Popularity Rank, Indian Political Parties

INTRODUCTION

India is the seventh-largest country by area, the second-most populous country, and the most populous democracy in the world. A Parliamentary Republic with a multi-party system, it has eight recognized national parties, including the Indian National Congress and the *Bharatiya Janata Party* (BJP), and more than 40 regional parties (India, 2019).

A political party is an organized group of people who have the same ideology, or who otherwise have the same political positions, and who field candidates for elections, in an attempt to get them elected and thereby implement the party's agenda. Political parties perform an important task in government. They bring people together to achieve control of the government, develop policies favorable to their interests or the groups that support them, and organize and persuade voters to elect their candidates to office.

In this present era websites plays the most vital role for information dissemination. Political parties have to disseminate and facilitate access to variety of information to their voters' (i.e. people) through their websites. The more people will come to know about the goals, objectives, plans, programmes, connectivity of the parties, the more they will have faith in those parties. That is the main reason why political parties need effective websites. From that point of view webometric evaluation of websites of the political parties is highly significant as this evaluation can suggest the ways of improvement to such websites.

LITERATURE REVIEW

The Web is increasingly used for political and social purposes and consequently has become an object of study in social sciences. In information science, webometric methods have been used to explore the social and political dimensions of the Web.

March (2006) suggests that in newer democracies in which political communication and political systems are less fixed and developed could allow a greater role for new technologies. This could be the case in Eastern European countries where democratic systems are very recent as a result of the past communist domination. E-campaigning and e-mobilization are also important areas of research, as the Internet has become a powerful tool to mobilize people.

Mukherjee's (2009) study was on applied webometric techniques to national political party's websites. It was an attempt to judge the popularity of Internet and to measure whether Internet can be used as a tool in Indian political context. Google, Yahoo and Alexa as tools of measurement have been used by the researcher. The study measures the popularity of political party's websites by analyzing links and using Wayback machine. That study compared the party's present website with its earlier view. The results indicated that political parties in India are using Internet as one of the viable tools for campaign and Internet can be used as a supplementary tool for measuring popularity.

OBJECTIVES

The objectives of the study are as follows:

- To calculate the simple, internal link and external link web impact factors of selected websites.
- To analyze the websites of political parties on the basis of SEO (search engine optimization).
- To find out the global popularity ranking of the websites.

SCOPE OF THE STUDY

The websites of 27 political parties (7 national and 20 state parties) in India have been considered for this webometric analysis. The table 4.1 represents the brief details of those political parties with their websites' domain extensions. According to the website of National Election Commission the ruling and opposition parties of various states have been selected along with the national parties.

Distribution of Domain Name Extensions

Domain name is a very important issue for any website. A domain suffix or 'top-level domain (TLD) is intended to define the type of website and it impacts on webpage visibility and SEO score. From the above table (Table 4.1) and the following figure (Figure 4.1) it can be concluded that out of 27 websites ten (10) websites have .org domain extension, nine (9) websites have .in domain extension, three (3) websites have .org.in domain extension, three (3) websites have .com domain extension and one (1) each website has .online and .net domain extension.

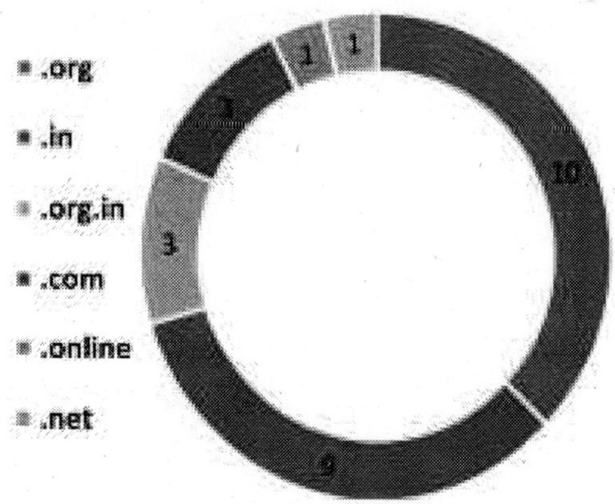

Fig. 4.1. Distribution of domain extensions

METHODOLOGY

Data have been collected from the websites of the 27 selected political parties' websites in India. For

Table 4.1. List of Selected Indian Political Parties Websites

Sl. No	Name of Political Party	URL	Abbvr.	Year of Establishment	Domain Extn.
	National Parties				
1	All India Trinamool Congress	http://aitcofficial.org/	AITMC	1998	.org
2	BahujanSamaj Party	http://www.bspindia.org/	BSP	1984	.org
3	BharatiyaJanata Party	https://www.bjp.org/hi	BJP	1980	.org
4	Communist Party of India	https://www.communistparty.in/	CPI	1925	.in
5	Communist Party of India (Marxist)	https://cpim.org/	CPI(M)	1964	.org
6	Indian National Congress	https://www.inc.in/en	INC	1885	.in
7	Nationalist Congress Party	https://www.ncp.org.in/	NCP	1999	.org.in
	State Parties				
8	AamAadmi Party	https://aamaadmiparty.org/	AAP	2012	.org
9	All India Anna Dravida Munnetra Kazhagam	http://www.supportaiadmk.org/	AIADMK	1972	.org
10	Biju Janata Dal	http://www.bjdodisha.org.in/home	BJD	1997	.org.in
11	Bodoland People's Front	http://www.bpfassam.in/	BPF	1985	.in
12	Dravida Munnetra Kazhagam	http://www.dmk.in/	DMK	1949	.in
13	Indian Union Muslim League	http://iuml.com/aboutiuml.html	IUML	1948	.com
14	Janata Dal (Secular)	http://jds.ind.in/	JD(S)	1999	.in
15	Janata Dal (United)	http://www.janatadalunited.online/	JD(U)	1999	.online
16	Jharkhand MuktiMorcha	https://jmmjharkhand.in/	JMM	1972	.in

17	Lok Janshakti Party	http://ljp.org.in/	LJP	2000	.org.in
18	Mizo National Front	http://mizonationalfront.org/	MNF	1959	.org
19	Naga People's Front	http://www.nagapeoplesfront.org/	NPF	2002	.org
20	People's Party of Arunachal	http://peoplespartyofarunachal.com/about-ppa//	PPA	1987	.com
21	Rashtriya Janata Dal	https://rjd.co.in/dev/	RJD	1997	.in
22	Samajwadi Party	https://www.samajwadiparty.in/	SP	1992	.in
23	ShiromaniAkali Dal	http://www.shiromaniakalidal.net/	SAD	1920	.net
24	Shiv Sena	https://shivsena.org/	SS	1966	.org
25	Sikkim KrantikariMorcha	http://sikkimdemocraticfront.in/	SKM	2013	.in
26	Telugu Desam Party	http://www.telugudesam.org/	TDP	1982	.org
27	YSR Congress Party	https://www.ysrcongress.com/	YSRCP	2011	.com

calculating three types of WIFs (simple, internal link and external link WIF) first the numbers of links have been counted from a link analyser tool named CleverStat (http://cleverstat.com/link-analyzer). For calculating the number of webpages of a particular website "site:domain name" syntax has been used as introduced by Ingwersen (1998). On the basis of these, the formula of calculating WIF as introduced by Ingwersen (1998) i.e. the ratio of the number of links to a site, to the number of webpages at the site, has been used. This can be stated thus:

A = Total number of webpages to a particular site

B = Total Number of Internal-links to a given site

C = Total Number of External links to a given site

D = Total number of links (External + Internal) to a site

Therefore, WIF (Simple) = **D/A**; WIF (Internal) = **B/A,** and WIF (External) = **C/A.**

In this study online SEO report generation tool, Neil Patel's SEO Analyzer (https://neilpatel.com/seo-analyzer/) has also been used to analyse and compare India's political party websites on various parameters like page size, load time, SEO score and speed score. For finding out the Indian and global popularity ranking of the selected websites Alexa (https://www.alexa.com/siteinfo) tool has been used.

DATA ANALYSIS AND FINDINGS

Calculation of Web Impact Factors (WIF)

The table 4.2 illustrates three types of WIF distribution of the selected Indian political party's websites with their webpage and link details.

Table 4.2 clearly denotes that according to the Simple Web Impact Factor (SWIF) ranking *Telugu Desam Party* (TDP) holds the numero uno status with SWIF of 1.128, while *Indian Union Muslim League* and *Shiv Sena* hold the 2nd and 3rd positions respectively with SWIFs of

Table 4.2. WIFs of Selected Indian Political Parties Websites

Name of the Political Party	*Number of Web Pages and Links*				*3 Types of Web Impact Factors*		
	Total No. of Webpage (A)	*Total No. of Internal-link (B)*	*Total No. of External-link (C)*	*Total No. of Links (D)*	*Simple WIF (D/A)*	*Internal-link WIF (B/A)*	*External-link WIF (C/A)*
AITMC	28,100	60	13	73	0.002	0.002	0.024
BSP	2030	27	53	80	0.039	0.013	0.026
BJP	11,400	91	45	136	0.011	0.007	0.003
CPI	229	6	5	11	0.048	0.026	0.021
CPI(M)	9070	54	5	59	0.006	0.005	5.512
INC	7970	83	12	95	0.011	0.011	0.001
NCP	3660	30	0	30	0.008	0.008	0
AAP	8680	104	26	130	0.014	0.011	0.002
AIADMK	4140	24	3	27	0.006	0.005	7.246
BJD	7890	27	12	39	0.004	0.003	0.001
BPF	127	9	4	13	0.102	0.070	0.031
DMK	701	27	14	41	0.058	0.038	0.019
IUML	25	14	0	14	0.56	0.56	0
JD(S)	1440	71	9	80	0.055	0.049	0.006
JD(U)	1070	61	18	79	0.073	0.057	0.016
JMM	143	11	9	20	0.139	0.076	0.062
LJP	73	10	2	12	0.164	0.136	0.027

MNF	44	3	0	3	0.75	0.75	0
NPF	59	7	4	11	0.186	0.118	0.067
PPA	113	9	5	14	0.123	0.079	0.044
RJD	100	23	7	30	0.3	0.23	0.07
SP	378	34	5	39	0.103	0.089	0.013
SAD	41	1	1	2	0.048	0.024	0.024
SS	139	20	12	32	0.230	0.143	0.086
SKM	149	19	9	28	0.187	0.127	0.060
TDP	39	40	4	44	1.128	1.025	0.102
YSRCP	9800	89	8	97	0.009	0.009	8.163

0.56and 0.230. According to Internal-link Web Impact Factor (IWIF) the previous three party websites hold the same 1st, 2nd and 3rd ranks with IWIFs of 1.025, 0.56and 0.143 respectively. In case of External-link Web Impact Factor (EWIF) YSR Congress Party holds the rank one position with EWIF of 8.163. AIADMK and CPI(M) hold the 2nd and 3rd positions with EWIFs of 7.246 and 5.512 respectively.

Results from SEO Analyzer

Web traffic is known as the collective number of visitors to a website. Search Engine Optimization increases the web traffic by making the website more visible to search engines (Sarkar, Pal & Kar, 2018). Table 4.3 depicts page size and load time of the Indian political party's websites. In the table 4.4 and figure 4.2 the Traffic Score, Speed Score and SEO Score of the websites have been depicted. Lok Janshakti Party website has the maximum loading time (32.21 seconds) which is not a good sign. AamAadmi Party website is the fastest to load its page in only 0.64 seconds. Lok Janshakti Party website has the maximum traffic score of 60. Nationalist Congress Party and *Rashtriya Janata Dal* both have the maximum SEO score of 89. Nationalist Congress Party again tops the list with maximum speed score of 85.

Table 4.3. Page Size and Load Time of the Websites

Political Party	*Page Size (KB/MB)*	*Load Time (Sec.)*	*Political Party*	*Page Size (KB/MB)*	*Load Time (Sec.)*
AITMC	426.7 KB	7.00	JD(U)	169.7 KB	7.95
BSP	842.6 KB	2.64	JMM	5.8 MB	2.94
BJP	149.5 KB	1.57	LJP	758.8 KB	32.21
CPI	410.2 KB	9.67	MNF	234.6 KB	6.17
CPI(M)	72.9 KB	1.96	NPF	512.4 KB	0.96
INC	764.9 KB	15.06	PPA	1.0 MB	2.74
NCP	33.5 KB	16.75	RJD	41.1 KB	3.58
AAP	744.4 KB	0.64	SP	348.2 KB	2.71
AIADMK	0.2 KB	14.35	SAD	645.1 KB	16.11

BJD	895.5 KB	7.82	SS	509.7 KB	7.21
BPF	543.6 KB	2.67	SKM	924.6 KB	30.09
DMK	117.8 KB	1.86	TDP	293.7 KB	14.64
IUML	69.7 KB	8.05	YSRCP	221.9 KB	5.02
JD(S)	985.0 KB	1.23			

Table 4.4. Traffic Score, Speed Score and SEO Score of the Websites

	Traffic score	*SEO score*	*Speed score*
All India Trinamool Congress	47	73	67
Bahujan Samaj Party	59	84	77
Bharatiya Janata Party	48	87	73
Communist Party of India	49	68	64
Communist Party of India (Marxist)	38	86	62
Indian National Congress	39	73	61
Nationalist Congress Party	30	89	85
Aam Aadmi Party	59	71	64
All India Anna Dravida Munnetra Kazhagam	36	86	63
Biju Janata Dal	53	66	64
Bodoland People's Front	58	88	67
DravidaMunnetraKazhagam	48	86	65
Indian Union Muslim League	44	68	77
Janata Dal (Secular)	58	67	61
Janata Dal (United)	47	66	70
Jharkhand Mukti Morcha	50	52	56
Lok Janshakti Party	60	85	62
Mizo National Front	39	72	58
Naga People's Front	46	84	58
People's Party of Arunachal	40	71	69
Rashtriya Janata Dal	0	89	83
Samajwadi Party	30	68	70
Shiromani Akali Dal	32	72	52
Shiv Sena	47	81	60
Sikkim Krantikari Morcha	48	62	54
Telugu Desam Party	30	70	82
YSR Congress Party	39	85	47

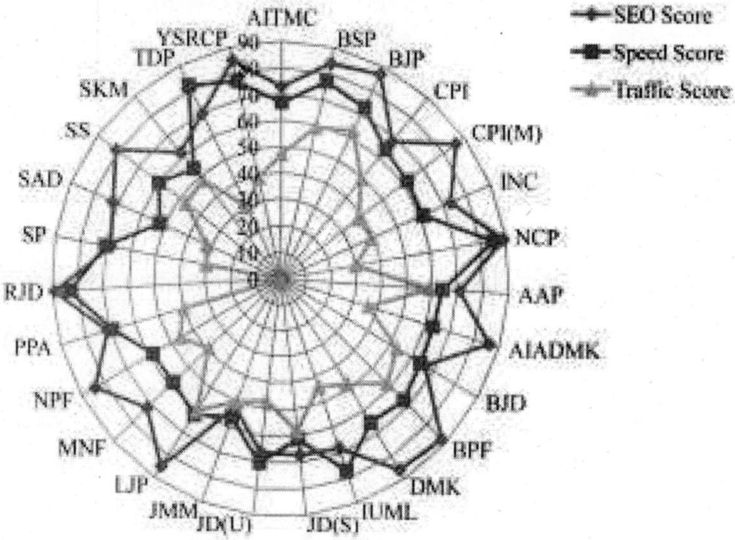

Fig. 4.2. SEO Analysis Scores

Popularity Rank of Websites

Website popularity ranking is another important indicator which helps for better promotion of a website. Ranking of a website is based on a combined measure of page views and unique site users. Popularity ranking of selected websites is portrayed through table 4.5.

Table 4.5. Popularity Ranking of the Websites

Political party	*Global rank*
AITMC	4,16,900
BSP	2,298,750
BJP	79,254
CPI	4,773,645
CPI(M)	618,447
INC	138,014
NCP	1,990,671
AAP	270,836
AIADMK	7,160,667
BJD	3,035,755
BPF	***

DMK	1,211,134
IUML	4,118,047
JD(S)	3,035,959
JD(U)	1,077,578
JMM	7,380,595
LJP	10,829,374
MNF	***
NPF	***
PPA	***
RJD	2,066,620
SP	1,211,861
SAD	***
SS	1,971,662
SKM	13, 838,460
TDP	1,266, 731
YSRCP	157,868

BJP websites ranks first among the Indian parties with a best global ranking of 79,254. It is followed by Indian National Congress and *YSR Congress Party* (with global ranking of 138,014 and 157,868 respectively).

CONCLUSION

Political parties in India are trying hard to impress the common mass through their websites. This quantitative analysis of the party websites upholds some of the qualities of these websites. While according to Simple Web Impact Factor (SWIF) and Internal-link Web Impact Factor (IWIF) ranking Telugu Desam Party (TDP) holds the numero uno status, in case of External-link Web Impact Factor (EWIF), YSR Congress Party holds the rank one position. Lok Janshakti Party website has the maximum loading time (32.21 seconds) which is not a good sign because the more delay in loading a website only adds to the annoyance of public. AamAadmi Party website is the fastest to load its page in only 0.64 seconds. Lok Janshakti Party website has the maximum traffic score of 60. Nationalist Congress Party and *Rashtriya*

Janata Dal both have the maximum SEO score of 89. Nationalist Congress Party again tops the list with maximum speed score of 85. BJP websites ranks first among the Indian parties with a global ranking of 79,254. It is followed by Indian National Congress and YSR Congress Party (with global ranking of 138,014 and 157,868 respectively). But it is not quite upto the mark considering the global rank. It only hints at the fact that Indian political party websites need to be improved.

REFERENCES

- *Alexa.* (n.d.). Retrieved August 20, 2019, from https://www.alexa.com/siteinfo
- Mukherjee, B. (2009). Link analysis of Indian political parties' web sites: A temporal comparison. *Annals of Library and Information Studies,* 56(September), 201-211.
- Bjorneborn, L. &Ingwersen P. (2004). Towards a basic framework for webometrics. *Journal of the American Society for Information Science and Technology, 55* (14), 1216- 1227. Retrieved August 14, 2019, from onlinelibrary.wiley.com/doi/10.1002/asi.20077/abstract
- India. (n.d.). In *Wikipedia.* Retrieved August 11, 2019 from https://en.wikipedia.org/wiki/India.
- Ingwersen, P. (1998). The calculation of web impact factors. *Journal of Documentation, 54* (2), 236-43.
- March, L. (2006). Virtual parties in a virtual world: Russian parties and the political internet. In S. Oates, D.M. Owen & R.K. Gibson (eds.), *The Internet and politics: Citizens, voters, and activists.* London: Routledge.
- Neilpatel. (n.d.). SEO analyzer. Retrieved August 21, 2019, from https://neilpatel.com/seo- analyzer/
- Sarkar, A., Pal, A., & Kar, S. (2018). Webometric mapping of tourism sites in India. *Library Philosophy and Practice (e-journal), 1957,* 1-14. Retrieved December 28, 2018 from http://digitalcommons.unl.edu/libphilprac/1957/

5

Webometric Analysis of Indian Banks

ABSTRACT

Web Impact Factor (WIF), Search Engine Optimization (SEO) ranking improve the visibility of a website's presence in online environment. The present study predominantly focuses on the WIFs of the Indian banking websites. On the basis of SEO (search engine optimization) effort has been made to measure the usability, performance, security of the websites, used headings, usage of images and alt tags, linking with social networking sites as well as to count the backlinks, page size, load time, request, traffic score, SEO score and speed score. Popularity ranking of the selected bank websites has also been done. Calculating three types of web impact factors it has been found that among the nationalised banks Indian Bank (IB) holds the numero uno status while among the private banks Lakshmi Vilas Bank Limited (LVB) holds the number one rank. On the basis of usability though nationalised banks enjoy better grades than their private counterparts, regarding SEO, performance and social linking private banks achieve higher grades. In the matter of security all the nationalised and private banks maintain grade A (including A+ and A-) security. Regarding ranking of websites Canara Bank holds the best global and Indian rank. Among the private banks HDFC Bank Limited holds the best global and Indian ranks.

Keywords : Web Impact Factor, WIF, Search Engine Optimization, SEO, Usability, Security, Popularity Rank, Indian Banks

INTRODUCTION

Present day world cannot keep a single step without the intervention of Internet. For the dissemination of information and spreading of communication web has played a significant role. Websites and web based user interfaces have become the window of communication in today's world. According to statistics, there are more than 2 billion Internet users in the world. Out of those, 137 million Internet users are from India (Kaur & Dani, 2014).

It only enhances the connectivity of the banks with millions of people by promoting banks to the larger portion of the society. Therefore, website is a vital cog of the banking activities. Though Internet banking in India is at its nascent stage but it is growing at a lightning fast speed. People of India are also showing interest in finding out the interest rates, present schemes, related forms and other documents from the websites of the banks rather than visiting the banks personally with the main motto of saving time and labour. In this paper, an effort has been made to evaluate the accessibility of the websites of Indian nationalised and private sector banks on the basis of a webometric analysis.

BANKING SYSTEM OF INDIA HEADED BY RESERVE BANK OF INDIA

Indian banking system is headed by the Reserve Bank of India (RBI). It is India's central banking institution, which controls the issuance and supply of the Indian rupee as well as played great role in controlling monetary policy in India and is responsible for monitoring the foreign exchange flows into the Indian economy by managing currency exchange rates and supervising how banks and non-banking financial institutions would function (Reserve Bank of India, n.d.). Indian banking system comprised of commercial, regional and cooperative banks. Commercial banks are divided into public sector and private sector banks. Public sector banks cover State Bank of India and its associates as well as other nationalized banks (Chand, n.d.). The present study encompasses these commercial banks (both public and private sector banks). In the following table 5.1 the selected nationalised and private banks have been delineated with their abbreviations (abbv.) and website URLs.

Table 5.1. Selected Nationalised and Private Banks

Bank Name	*Abbv.*	*URL*
	Nationalised Banks	
Allahabad Bank	ALB	https://www.allahabadbank.in/
Andhra Bank	ADB	https://www.andhrabank.in/english/home.aspx
Bank of Baroda	BOB	https://www.bankofbaroda.com/
Bank of India	BOI	https://www.bankofindia.co.in/english/home.aspx
Bank of Maharashtra	BOM	https://www.bankofmaharashtra.in/
Canara Bank	CB	https://www.canarabank.in/
Central Bank of India	CBI	https://www.centralbank.net.in/jsp/startMain.jsp
Corporation Bank	COB	https://www.corpbank.com/
Dena Bank	DB	https://www.denabank.com/
Indian Bank	IB	http://www.indianbank.in/
Indian Overseas Bank	IOB	https://www.iob.in/
Oriental Bank of Commerce	OBC	https://www.obcindia.co.in/
Punjab & Sind Bank	PSB	https://www.psbindia.com/
Punjab National Bank	PNB	https://www.pnbindia.in/
State Bank of India	SBI	https://sbi.co.in/
Syndicate Bank	SYB	www.syndicatebank.in/english/home.aspx
UCO Bank	UCO	https://www.ucobank.com/english/home.aspx
Union Bank of India	UBOI	https://www.unionbankofindia.co.in/english/home.aspx
United Bank Of India	UBI	https://www.unitedbankofindia.com/english/home.aspx

Vijaya Bank	VB	https://www.vijayabank.com/
	Private Banks	
Axis Bank Limited	AXB	https://www.axisbank.com/
Bandhan Bank Limited	BB	https://www.bandhanbank.com/
Catholic Syrian Bank Limited	CSB	https://www.csb.co.in/
City Union Bank Limited	CUB	https://www.cityunionbank.com/
DCB Bank Limited	DCB	https://www.dcbbank.com/
Dhanlaxmi Bank Limited	DLXB	https://www.dhanbank.com/
Federal Bank Limited	FB	https://www.federalbank.co.in/
HDFC Bank Limited	HDFC	https://www.hdfcbank.com/
ICICI Bank Limited	ICICI	https://www.icicibank.com/
IndusInd Bank Limited	IB	https://www.indusind.com/
IDFC Bank Limited	IDFC	https://www.idfcbank.com/
Jammu & Kashmir Bank Limited	JKB	https://www.jkbank.com/
Karnataka Bank Limited	KB	https://karnatakabank.com/
Karur Vysya Bank Limited	KVB	https://www.kvb.co.in/
Kotak Mahindra Bank Limited	KM	https://www.kotak.com/en.html
Lakshmi Vilas Bank Limited	LVB	https://www.lvbank.com/
Nainital Bank Limited	NB	www.nainitalbank.co.in/
RBL Bank Limited	RBL	https://www.rblbank.com/
South Indian Bank Limited	SIB	https://www.southindianbank.com/
Tamilnad Mercantile Bank Limited	TMB	https://www.tmb.in/
YES Bank Limited	YB	https://www.yesbank.in/

LITERATURE REVIEW

Webometrics is the study of the quantitative aspects of construction and the use of information resources, structures and technologies on the web, based upon bibliometric and informetric approaches. According to Bjorneborn and Ingwersen, a webometric study basically covers the main four areas: Web page content analysis; Web link structure analysis (self link, external link etc.); Web usage analysis (searching and browsing behavior) and Web technology analysis (search engine performance) (Bjorneborn and Ingwersen, 2004). WIF is the part of the methodology in webometric studies. The WIF provides quantitative tools for ranking, evaluating, categorizing and comparing the websites (Noruzi, 2005). Kaur and Dani (2014) have evaluated accessibility of banking websites. Their objective was to analyze the status of accessibility of banking websites as it allows people with disabilities to be independent and more in control of their own financial requirements. For their study, website of Indian banks were chosen. The results of the evaluation indicated that the situation of website accessibility of Indian banking websites is not very satisfactory in terms of number of errors reported by the automatic tools (Kaur & Dani, 2014). As not much work has been found regarding webometric analysis of Indian banks, the present study has been conducted.

OBJECTIVES

The objectives of the study are as follows:

- To calculate three types of web impact factors (WIF) of India's nationalised and private bank websites, namely simple web impact factor, self link or inlink web impact factor and external link web impact factor.
- To analyse the websites of Indian nationalised and private banks under Reserve Bank of India on the basis of SEO (search engine optimization) especially to measure the usability, performance, security of the websites, used headings, usage of images and alt tags, linking with social networking sites as well as to count the backlinks, page size, load time, request, traffic score, SEO score and speed score.
- To find out the global popularity ranking of the

banks' websites on the basis of Alexa ranking.

SCOPE AND LIMITATIONS

Twenty nationalised banks and twenty one private banks have been selected from the website of Reserve Bank of India for this study (Reserve Bank of India, n.d.). The present study has been restricted within the particular time period i.e. from 15/11/2018 to 31/12/2018. As CleverStat tool fails to count the number of inlinks and external links of Central Bank of India, Corporation Bank, Oriental Bank of Commerce, Syndicate Bank, Vijaya Bank, Catholic Syrian Bank Limited, City Union Bank Limited and HDFC Bank, these banks have been kept outside the purview of web impact factor calculation.

METHODOLOGY

At first, websites with URLs of 20 nationalised banks and 21 private banks have been selected from the list of RBI. For three types of WIF calculation at first total number of webpages for each website have been collected from the Google search engine (which have large database) using the command "site:domain name" introduced by Ingwersen (1998). For the number of inlinks and external links counting, a link analyser tool named CleverStat (http://cleverstat.com/link-analyzer) has been used. Then data have been collected from SEO tool SEOptimer (https://www.seoptimer.com/) for analysing websites from different angles. Then the selected bank websites are observed and analysed with the help of online Search Engine Optimization (SEO) tools like Neil Patel's SEO analyser (https://neilpatel.com/seo-analyzer/) and Alexa (https://www.alexa.com/siteinfo). After data collection, the collected data were analysed and tabulated keeping in view the objective of the study.

DATA ANALYSIS AND FINDINGS

Calculation of Web Impact Factors (WIF)

Web impact factor or WIF is the web version of impact factor. There are three types of WIFs: Simple Web Impact Factor, Internal link Web Impact Factor (also known as Self link Web Impact Factor) and External link Web Impact Factor. The WIF introduced by Ingwersen (1998) is the ratio of the number of links to a site, to the number of webpages at the site. This can be stated thus:

A = Total number of webpages to a particular site

B = Total Number of Internal links to a given site

C = Total Number of External links to a given site

D = Total number of links (External + Internal) to a site

Therefore, WIF (simple) = **D/A**; WIF (Internal) = **B/A,** and WIF (External) = **C/A.**

The table 5.2 illustrates the three types of WIF distribution of bank websites with their webpage and link details.

Table 5.2. WIFs of Selected Bank Websites

Banks	*Number of Web Pages and Links*				*3 Types of Web Impact Factors*		
	Total No. of Web-page (A)	*Total No. of Internal-links (B)*	*Total No. of External links (C)*	*Total No. of Links (D)*	*Simple WIF (D/A)*	*Internal link WIF (B/A)*	*External link WIF (C/A)*
National							
ALB	3880	95	21	116	0.029	0.024	0.005
ADB	2750	226	30	256	0.093	0.082	0.010
BOB	13700	344	53	397	0.028	0.025	0.003
BOI	5750	241	8	249	0.043	0.041	0.001
BOM	7760	126	14	140	0.018	0.016	0.001
CB	261	10	24	34	0.130	0.038	0.091
DB	3640	191	12	203	0.055	0.052	0.003
IB	934	151	92	243	0.260	0.161	0.098
IOB	3970	285	22	307	0.077	0.071	0.005

PSB	1590	246	17	263	0.165	0.154	0.010
PNB	2160	153	34	187	0.086	0.070	0.015
SBI	17500	95	35	130	0.007	0.005	0.002
UCO	2570	107	21	128	0.049	0.041	0.008
UBOI	8210	128	20	148	0.018	0.015	0.002
UBI	2790	100	27	127	0.045	0.035	0.009
Private							
AXB	29400	258	74	332	0.011	0.008	0.002
BB	464	52	5	57	0.122	0.112	0.010
DCB	2450	54	7	61	0.024	0.022	0.002
DLXB	1320	89	5	94	0.071	0.067	0.003
FB	4530	234	25	259	0.057	0.051	0.005
ICICI	31300	220	44	264	0.008	0.006	0.001
IB	31300	257	13	270	0.008	0.008	0.0004
IDFC	4960	153	17	170	0.034	0.030	0.003
JKB	1360	221	13	234	0.172	0.162	0.009
KB	2080	193	13	206	0.099	0.092	0.006
KVB	1230	29	4	33	0.026	0.023	0.003
KM	15400	171	32	203	0.013	0.011	0.002
LVB	8	85	20	105	13.125	10.625	2.5
NB	926	0	0	0	0	0	0
RBL	5720	0	0	0	0	0	0
SIB	4640	222	14	236	0.050	0.047	0.003
TMB	3650	28	14	42	0.011	0.007	0.003
YB	205000	242	12	254	0.001	0.001	0.00005

On the basis of simple web impact factor Indian Bank (IB) holds the numero uno status among the nationalised banks with 0.260 but among the private banks Lakshmi Vilas Bank Limited (LVB) holds the number one rank with an impact factor of 13.125. This LVB also holds the 1st position among private as well as nationalised banks considering its internal link and external link web impact factors with 10.625 and 2.5 respectively. In case of these two types of web impact factors (internal and external) Indian Bank (IB) again holds the 1st position among nationalised banks with 0.161 and 0.098 respectively.

Overall Grade Analysis of Indian Bank Websites in Various Categories

Following table shows the overall grade wise analysed results of selected Indian bank websites through online SEOptimer tool (https://www.seoptimer.com/). This table has focused on five parameters: SEO, Usability, Performance, Social and Security.

Search engine optimization (SEO) is the process of optimizing the website content such as metatag, page size, load time, images, text etc. and finally optimizing a whole website for improving their search engine rankings. Usability maximizes website's audience and minimizes user bounce rates (which can indirectly affect search engine rankings). It is important to make a website mobile and tablet friendly as today the majority of web traffic comes from these sources. Performance is also vital to ensure a good user experience. Social activity is another essential parameter for user communication, brand awareness and as a promotional channel to bring more visitors to a website. Finally the security parameter ensures how a website protects user data or safeguards against data loss (SEOptimer, n.d.). The following table reflects that on the basis of SEO Central Bank of India is the only nationalised bank to achieve grade A+ whereas Dhanlaxmi Bank Limited, HDFC Bank Limited and ICICI Bank Limited are the three private banks to achieve grade A+. On the basis of Usability 15 nationalised banks have got A grade whereas only 11 private banks achieve grade A (including A-). Performance status of nationalised banks are not up to the mark in comparison to their private counter parts as only Andhra Bank and United Bank of India receive A- grade whereas Axis Bank Limited (A), Nainital Bank Limited(A-), Tamilnad Mercantile Bank Ltd. (A+), YES Bank Limited (A-) hit grade A category. Only three nationalised banks have grade A in Social linking whereas for private banks the number is seven. But regarding Security all the nationalised and private banks maintain grade A (including A+ and A-) security.

Table 5.3. Overall Grade Analysis of Indian Bank Websites in Various Categories

Bank Name (Nationalised Banks)	*Overall Grade in Various Categories* SEO	*Usability*	*Performance*	*Social*	*Security*
Allahabad Bank	C-	A	C+	B-	A+
Andhra Bank	B	A	A-	B-	A+
Bank of Baroda	B	A	C+	B+	A+
Bank of India	B-	A	B+	B-	A+
Bank of Maharashtra	B-	D	C+	D-	A+
Canara Bank	D+	A	C+	D-	A+
Central Bank of India	A+	F-	C+	B+	—
Corporation Bank	C-	A	B-	D-	A-
Dena Bank	D+	A	D	D-	A+
Indian Bank	A-	A	D	A-	A+
Indian Overseas Bank	D+	B-	C+	C+	A+
Oriental Bank of Commerce	—	F-	C+	—	A+
Punjab & Sind Bank	B	A	D+	C-	A+
Punjab National Bank	B-	A	B-	B-	A+
State Bank of India	D+	B+	B-	A+	A-
Syndicate Bank	C+	A	B+	B	A+
UCO Bank	D+	A	B	D-	A-
Union Bank of India	B-	A	C	A-	A+
United Bank of India	D+	A	A-	B-	A-
Vijaya Bank	B-	A	B	D	A+
Private Banks					
Axis Bank Limited	C	A	A	A-	A-
Bandhan Bank Limited	B	B+	C	B	A+
Catholic Syrian Bank Ltd.	—	A-	E+	—	A+
City Union Bank Limited	—	F-	C+	—	A+
DCB Bank Limited	D+	A	B-	B	A+
Dhanlaxmi Bank Limited	A+	F-	C+	—	A+
Federal Bank Limited	B	A	C	B-	A+
HDFC Bank Limited	A+	A-	B	—	A+
ICICI Bank Limited	A+	A	D	B-	A+
IndusInd Bank Limited	B	B+	B	A	A+
IDFC Bank Limited	B-	B+	B	A-	A+
Jammu & Kashmir Bank Limited	B-	B+	B	A	A+

Karnataka Bank Limited	C	A	D	A	A-
Karur Vysya Bank Limited	B+	E+	B-	D-	A+
Kotak Mahindra Bank Limited	B	A	B+	A	A+
Lakshmi Vilas Bank Limited	C-	D	C	C-	A-
Nainital Bank Limited	C	D+	A-	D-	A+
RBL Bank Limited	B-	A	B-	B-	A+
South Indian Bank Limited	C	A	D+	A-	A+
Tamilnad Mercantile Bank Ltd.	C-	D+	A+	B+	A-
YES Bank Limited	B+	A	A-	B+	A+

Depending on the grades on different categories of Kotak Mahindra Bank Limited website, the following graphic diagram has been drawn with the help of the SEOptimer tool. The outer red line of the diagram indicates when all five parameters are in Grade A+. According to the above table not a single bank website could reach the fully expanded diagram as like the outer diagram of following figure. Some websites are very much poor in their grade results.

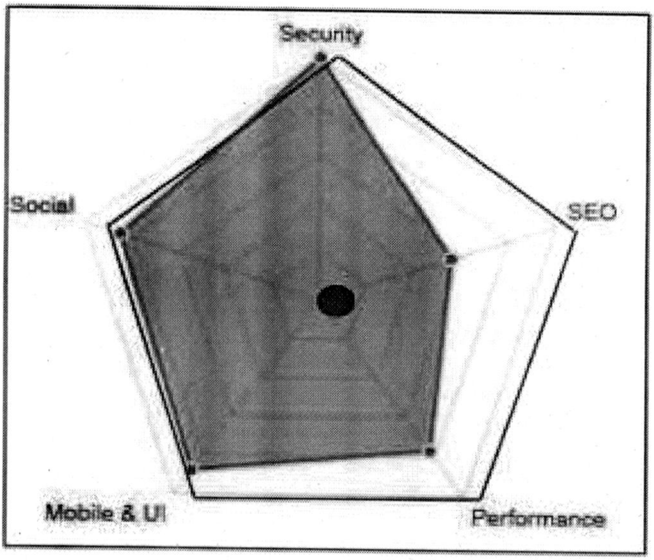

Fig. 5.1. Kotak Mahindra Bank Limited Website

Distribution of Header Tag

In webpage designing HTML defines six levels of headings defined by <h1> to <h6> tag. <h1> tag defines largest heading and <h6> defines smallest heading. These tags are important indicators to search engines for defining the important content topics of a web page, and subsequently the keywords it should rank for (SEOptimer, n.d.). The following table depicts the bank wise distribution of tags from <h1> to <h6>. Central Bank of India, Oriental Bank of Commerce, Catholic Syrian Bank Limited, City Union Bank Limited, Dhanlaxmi Bank Limited, HDFC Bank Limited have been kept outside for this calculation as SEOptimer tool could not find any result for these banks. From this table it has been found that only ICICI Bank website has all types of headings pointing at the proper distribution of headings for matters of different importance.

Table 5.4. Distribution of Header Tags

Bank Name	*Header Tags*					
	H1	*H2*	*H3*	*H4*	*H5*	*H6*
Nationalised Banks						
Allahabad Bank	0	14	13	0	0	0
Andhra Bank	1	0	0	0	0	0
Bank of Baroda	0	7	13	0	0	0
Bank of India	0	5	18	0	0	0
Bank of Maharashtra	0	0	0	0	0	0
Canara Bank	0	0	0	0	0	0
Corporation Bank	1	1	35	24	0	0
Dena Bank	0	0	0	0	0	0
Indian Bank	9	0	3	2	0	0
Indian Overseas Bank	0	0	0	0	0	0
Punjab & Sind Bank	0	9	65	0	1	0
Punjab National Bank	0	0	40	5	1	0
State Bank of India	0	6	74	118	0	0
Syndicate Bank	1	0	0	0	0	0
UCO Bank	0	0	29	7	0	0
Union Bank of India	1	2	26	4	1	0

United Bank of India	0	0	0	0	0	0
Vijaya Bank	0	8	0	0	0	0
Private Banks						
Axis Bank Limited	0	15	41	10	1	0
Bandhan Bank Limited	7	0	5	0	0	0
DCB Bank Limited	4	0	0	0	0	0
Federal Bank Limited	1	12	71	5	0	1
ICICI Bank Limited	1	14	1	1	52	4
IndusInd Bank Limited	1	13	15	4	0	0
IDFC Bank Limited	1	0	0	40	0	0
Jammu & Kashmir Bank Limited	0	0	0	30	0	0
Karnataka Bank Limited	10	12	4	0	0	0
Karur Vysya Bank Limited	0	5	0	0	0	0
Kotak Mahindra Bank Limited	1	8	29	45	0	0
Lakshmi Vilas Bank Limited	0	0	0	0	0	0
Nainital Bank Limited	0	0	0	0	0	0
RBL Bank Limited	0	0	1	5	0	0
South Indian Bank Limited	0	0	0	0	0	0
Tamilnad Mercantile Bank Limited	0	2	22	0	0	0
YES Bank Limited	1	34	2	22	0	0

Distribution of Image and ALT Tag

The HTML 'alt' attribute specifies an alternate text for an image, if the image could not be displayed. The alt attribute provides alternative information for an image if a user for some reason fails to view it (because of slow Internet connection or any other). So if anyone is using an image as a button to buy product X, the alt text should say: "button to buy product X". Image alt attribute is very essential for any kind of website (SEOptimer, n.d.). The following table draws the distribution of number of images and present 'alt' tag for those images. Only those banks have been included in this table (5.5) on which information is available in the SEOptimer tool.

Table 5.5. Distribution of Image ALT Tag

Bank Name	*Images and ALT Tag*		
	No of Images	*ALT Tag present*	*Percentage*
	Nationalised Banks		
Allahabad Bank	56	24	42.85%
Andhra Bank	22	21	95.45%
Bank of Baroda	26	26	100%
Bank of India	58	57	98.27%
Bank of Maharashtra	90	0	0%
Corporation Bank	81	2	2.46%
Dena Bank	62	35	56.45%
Indian Bank	56	4	7.14%
Indian Overseas Bank	73	45	61.64%
Punjab & Sind Bank	94	90	95.74%
Punjab National Bank	62	58	93.54%
State Bank of India	27	7	25.92%
Syndicate Bank	46	35	76.08%
UCO Bank	86	80	93.02%
Union Bank of India	97	55	56.70%
United Bank of India	45	42	93.33%
Vijaya Bank	40	4	10%
	Private Banks		
Axis Bank Limited	31	14	45.16%
Bandhan Bank Limited	24	22	61.66%
DCB Bank Limited	9	8	88.88%
Federal Bank Limited	54	37	68.51%
ICICI Bank Limited	125	52	41.6%
IndusInd Bank Limited	44	35	79.54%
IDFC Bank Limited	55	12	21.81%
Jammu & Kashmir Bank Limited	16	1	6.25%
Karnataka Bank Limited	63	63	100%
Karur Vysya Bank Limited	21	6	28.57%
Kotak Mahindra Bank Limited	66	58	87.87%
Lakshmi Vilas Bank Limited	41	5	12.19%
Nainital Bank Limited	18	6	33.33%

RBL Bank Limited	49	30	61.22%
South Indian Bank Limited	38	18	47.36%
Tamilnad Mercantile Bank Limited	11	11	100%
YES Bank Limited	35	10	28.57%

The above table clearly indicates that Bank of Baroda, Karnataka Bank Limited and Tamilnad Mercantile Bank Limited enjoy 100% parity between image and its alternative 'alt' attributes. Six numbers of nationalised banks are having more than 90% (but less than 100%) parity between images and 'alt' tags whereas this number is zero for private banks.

Connection with Social Media

Previously it has been mentioned that activity in social media is essential for user communication. It enhances the brand value and is used as a promotional channel to bring more users to a website (SEOptimer, n.d.). Following table represents various bank websites' link with social networking sites. Only those banks have been included in this table on which information is available in the SEOptimer tool.

Table 5.6. Distribution of Connectivity with Social Media, Social Sharing and Followers

Bank Name	*Connectivity with Social Media, Social Sharing and Followers*					
	Facebook share	*Google+*	*Linked-In*	*Printe-rest*	*You Tube*	*Twitter follower*
National						
ALB	1956	0	0	0	0	2332
ADB	2607	0	0	0	0	10592
BOB	6374	0	0	0	0	61246
BOI	2986	0	0	0	0	5728
BOM	2644	0	0	0	0	0
CB	371	0	0	0	0	0
COB	734	0	0	0	0	0
DB	2051	0	0	0	0	0

IB	2668	0	0	0	3819	10020
IOB	2688	0	0	0	2609	6402
PSB	1106	0	0	0	0	295
PNB	3008	0	0	0	0	62305
SBI	1041	0	0	0	186746	3684969
SYB	2938	0	0	0	2	2288
UCO	893	0	0	0	0	0
UBOI	2865	0	0	0	7422	61239
UBI	1787	0	0	0	0	1988
VB	2002	0	0	0	0	0
(Private)						
AXB	16147	0	0	0	41280	276777
BB	2987	0	0	0	7115	11226
DCB	1102	0	0	0	0	1325
FB	9252	0	0	0	0	7497
ICICI	462311	0	0	7	0	476999
IB	10415	1292	0	202	13192	59630
IDFC	2551	0	0	2	8662	56844
JKB	802	0	0	0	512	5513
KB	257	0	0	0	2020	4253
KVB	1104	0	0	0	0	0
KM	41150	19357	0	1	100779	223541
LVB	2563	0	0	3	0	0
NB	327	0	0	0	0	0
RBL	147233	0	0	0	0	227777
SIB	1969	309	0	0	1767	3707
TMB	1291	300	0	0	0	510
YB	16815	0	0	0	6568	1753176

From the above table it is evident that only some private banks have links to Google+, LinkedIn and Pinterest. Bank of Baroda has the largest amount of Facebook share (6374) among the nationalised banks. ICICI Bank with 462311 Facebook share tops the list amidst both the private and nationalised banks. State Bank of India has the largest amount of linking with Youtube (regarding video sharing and such other things) with 186746 among the nationalised banks as well as private banks and this number is 100779 for Kotak Mahindra Bank Limited which holds the 2nd rank amidst all banks. State Bank of India with 3684969 Twitter followers holds the numero uno status among all the banks whereas Yes Bank, with1753176 followers is at the 2nd position among all the banks. So in the field of social connectivity State Bank of India or SBI really establishes its supremacy.

Results from SEO Analyzer

Web traffic is known as the collective number of visitors to a website. Search Engine Optimization increases the web traffic by making the website more visible to search engines (Sarkar, Pal & Kar, 2018). In this study online SEO report generation tool, Neil Patel's SEO Analyzer (https://neilpatel.com/seo-analyzer/) has been used to analyse and compare India's nationalised and private bank websites on various parameters like backlinks, page size, load time, request, traffic score, SEO score and speed score. The table below depicts these aforesaid features of Indian banking sites with the scores. Only those banks have been included in this table on which information is available from the SEO Analyzer tool.

Table 5.7. Scores via SEO Analyzer

	Back links	*Page size (KB/MB)*	*Load time (Sec.)*	*Req-uest*	*Traffic Score*	*SEO Score*	*Speed score*
		Nationalised Banks					
Allahabad Bank	233	940.0KB	23.23	70	55	61	63
Andhra Bank	872	623.0KB	5.32	71	60	81	61
Bank of Baroda	1513	951.5KB	5.68	50	60	77	63
Bank of India	971	1.7KB	2.52	2	60	68	85
Bank of Maharashtra	1067	2.1MB	8.87	111	50	85	47
Canara Bank	139	706.1KB	60.06	45	67	72	62
Central Bank of India	216	112.2KB	6.31	29	62	65	65
Dena Bank	1022	1.4MB	12.19	71	50	69	75
Indian Bank	1367	3.2MB	10.81	152	58	85	52

Indian Overseas Bank	809	2.2MB	11.57	67	56	67	58
Punjab & Sind Bank	468	1.8MB	14.43	133	50	63	63
Punjab National Bank	461	1.1MB	10.71	84	57	67	56
State Bank of India	2164	620.9KB	5.59	53	57	31	59
Syndicate Bank	855	2.8MB	14.36	246	60	81	66
UCO Bank	730	3.3MB	9.36	149	55	59	50
Union Bank of India	1645	1.8MB	7.39	156	60	78	53
United Bank of India	798	23.1KB	1.62	5	60	73	74
Vijaya Bank	915	379.9KB	4.72	64	56	79	61
Private Banks							
Axis Bank Limited	1293	1.8MB	1.76	66	70	63	73
Bandhan Bank Limited	141	2.1MB	7.04	77	55	86	57
DCB Bank Limited	202	177.3KB	10.17	34	55	81	64
Federal Bank Limited	649	657.4KB	12.58	113	58	45	63
ICICI Bank Limited	2057	7.1MB	120.05	815	77	63	51
IndusInd Bank Limited	648	1.4MB	7.57	110	63	70	62
IDFC Bank Limited	147	2.3MB	4.06	114	59	59	62
Jammu & Kashmir Bank Limited	87	660.0KB	2.46	69	55	69	77
Karnataka Bank Limited	448	992.3KB	6.56	70	54	61	74
Karur Vysya Bank Limited	571	1.5MB	5.09	75	59	82	60
Kotak Mahindra Bank Limited	1178	1.8MB	7.18	89	69	60	59
Lakshmi Vilas Bank Limited	551	894.8KB	6.58	102	50	70	52
Nainital Bank Limited	444	0.4KB	0.51	1	64	74	81
RBL Bank Limited	177	407.2KB	3.63	38	60	69	67
South Indian Bank Limited	668	1.5MB	3.73	83	59	76	73
Tamilnad Mercantile Bank Limited	367	150.4KB	3.61	15	49	85	90
YES Bank Limited	1358	1.1MB	2.36	64	65	70	68

The above table shows that State Bank of India has

the largest amount of backlinks (2164) among all the banks. ICICI Bank Limited website is the heaviest website with 7.1 MB page size. Consequently this website takes the maximum load time i.e. 120.05 second. This bank also has the largest amount of requests i.e. 805 and maximum traffic score i.e. 77. Bandhan Bank Limited has the highest SEO score i.e. 86. Tamilnad Mercantile Bank Limited tops the list of all banks with a speed score of 90.

Popularity Rank of Bank Websites

Website popularity ranking is another important indicator which helps to better promotion of a website. Ranking of a website is based on a combined measure of page views and unique site users (Sarkar, Pal & Kar, 2018). Popularity rankings of selected bank websites have been depicted below through the following table.

Table 5.8. Popularity Rank of the Bank Websites

Bank Name	*Alexa Ranking*	
	Global	*Indian*
	Nationalised Banks	
Allahabad Bank	63,666	4,774
Andhra Bank	14,970	1,063
Bank of Baroda	18,454	1,415
Bank of India	10680	742
Bank of Maharashtra	79699	8167
Canara Bank	4810	328
Central Bank of India	9529	671
Corporation Bank	41,577	2969
Dena Bank	128124	8985
Indian Bank	30792	2216
Indian Overseas Bank	58873	4571
Oriental Bank of Commerce	135,275	8954
Punjab & Sind Bank	110822	7956
Punjab National Bank	32891	3253
State Bank of India	4,930	345
Syndicate Bank	17317	1196
UCO Bank	70973	4778

Union Bank of India	13165	1117
United Bank of India	13324	879
Vijaya Bank	46120	4094
	Private Banks	
Axis Bank Limited	1,635	120
Bandhan Bank Limited	63,340	4,359
Catholic Syrian Bank Limited	456,845	32,368
City Union Bank Limited	111,070	7,852
DCB Bank Limited	69,046	5,355
Dhanlaxmi Bank Limited	271,377	22,463
Federal Bank Limited	28,876	3,020
HDFC Bank Limited	370	18
ICICI Bank Limited	512	29
IndusInd Bank Limited	8,394	568
IDFC Bank Limited	25,698	1,771
Jammu & Kashmir Bank Limited	65,266	5,659
Karnataka Bank Limited	81,263	5,422
Karur Vysya Bank Limited	26,230	1,779
Kotak Mahindra Bank Limited	2,952	209
Lakshmi Vilas Bank Limited	134,695	6,647
Nainital Bank Limited	494,307	40,781
RBL Bank Limited	17,423	1,195
South Indian Bank Limited	25,780	1,950
Tamilnad Mercantile Bank Limited	218,999	18,891
YES Bank Limited	6,700	452

The above table clearly points out that among the nationalised banks Canara Bank holds the best global rank i.e. 4810 and it has the best Indian rank also i.e. 328. This bank is followed by State Bank of India in both the global and Indian ranking i.e. 4930 and 345 respectively. Among the private banks HDFC Bank Limited holds the best global and Indian ranks i.e. 370 and 18 respectively. It is also the best among both the nationalised and private banks.

CONCLUSION

Throughout this webometric analyse websites of Indian banks have got an overall reflection. Calculating three types of web impact factors it has been found that among the nationalised banks Indian Bank (IB) holds the numero uno status while among the private banks Lakshmi Vilas Bank Limited (LVB) holds the number one rank. LVB also ranks first among both the nationalised and private banks in this field. On the basis of usability though nationalised banks enjoy better grades than their private counterparts, regarding SEO, performance and social linking private banks achieve higher grades. In the matter of security all the nationalised and private banks maintain grade A (including A+ and A-) security. Though in the field of social connectivity via social networking, private banks are slightly ahead of the nationalised banks but State Bank of India or SBI with its large amount of Youtube links and Twitter followers really moves with its head held high. The SEO analyzer tool's statistics define that State Bank of India has the largest amount of backlinks (2164) among all the banks. ICICI Bank Limited website is the heaviest website with 7.1 MB page size. Consequently this website takes the maximum load time i.e. 120.05 second. This bank also has the largest amount of requests i.e. 805 and maximum traffic score i.e. 77. Bandhan Bank Limited has the highest SEO score i.e. 86. Tamilnad Mercantile Bank Limited tops the list of all banks with a speed score of 90. Regarding ranking of websites Canara Bank holds the best global rank i.e. 4810 and it has the best Indian rank also i.e. 328. This bank is followed by State Bank of India in both the global and Indian ranking i.e. 4930 and 345 respectively. Among the private banks HDFC Bank Limited holds the best global and Indian ranks i.e. 370 and 18 respectively. It is also the best among both the nationalised and private banks.

REFERENCES

- *Alexa.* (n.d.). Retrieved December 20, 2018, from https://www.alexa.com/siteinfo
- Bjorneborn, L. &Ingwersen P. (2004). Towards a basic framework for webometrics. *Journal of the American Society for Information Science and Technology, 55* (14), 1216-1227. Retrieved December 14, 2018, from onlinelibrary.wiley.com/doi/10.1002/asi.20077/abstract
- Chand, S. (n.d.). Indian banking system: Structure and other details (with diagrams). In *Your Article Library.* Retrieved December 16, 2018, from http://www.yourarticlelibrary.com/banking/indian banking-system-structure-and-other-details-with-diagrams/23495
- Kaur, A. & Dani, D. (2014). Banking websites in India: An accessibility evaluation. *CSI Transaction on ICT, 2*(1), 23-34. Retrieved from https://link.springer.com/article/10.1007/s40012-014-0040-x
- Ingwersen, P. (1998). The calculation of web impact factors. *Journal of Documentation, 54* (2), 236-43.
- Neilpatel. (n.d.). SEO analyzer. Retrieved December 20, 2018, from https://neilpatel.com/seo-analyzer/
- Noruzi, A. (2005). Web impact factors for Iranian universities. *Webology, 2*(1). Retrieved December 14, 2018, from http://www.webology.ir/2005/v2n1/a11.html
- Reserve Bank of India.(n.d.). In *Wikipedia.* Retrieved December 18, 2018, from https://en.wikipedia.org/wiki/Reserve_Bank_of_India
- *Reserve Bank of India.* (n.d.). Retrieved December 18, 2018, from https://rbi.org.in/CommonPerson/english/scripts/banksinindia.aspx
- *SEOptimer.* (n.d.). Retrieved December 18, 2018, from https://www.seoptimer.com/
- Sarkar, A., Pal, A., & Kar, S. (2018). Webometric mapping of tourism sites in India. *Library Philosophy and Practice (e-journal),* 1-14. Retrieved December 28, 2018 from http://digitalcommons.unl.edu/libphilprac/1957/

6

Content Analysis of Asian National Library Websites

ABSTRACT

Libraries are slowly shifting their role from being custodians of collection-based traditional information resources to being providers of access-based digital information resources. National library being the apex body of a country's library system really holds a vital part in the whole gamut of knowledge sharing. Library websites play an important role for this purpose. The basic purpose of this study is to analyze the contents of national library websites of Asian countries. An evaluation method was carried out for this study to know the how far the websites of national libraries of Asian countries had satisfied the selected parameters as instructed in the respective guidelines. According to findings, 9% of selected national library websites regardless of their characteristics had fallen in the grade of "A++", 44% had fallen in "A" and remaining 47% had been considered in the grade of "B".

Keywords: Traditional information resources, Digital information resources, National library, NL, Content analysis

INTRODUCTION

Library and information centers are the vital part of the world's education and information storage and retrieval system. All kinds of people including students, teachers, business executives, government officials, scholars, and scientists use library resources for their purposes. A national library (NL) is a library specifically established by the government of a country to serve as the preeminent repository of information for that country. A national library is that library which has the duty of collecting and preserving the literature of the nation within and outside the country. Thus, national libraries are those libraries whose community is the nation at large. A national library reflects the cultural heritage of the nation. It preserves the information for future generation. It also plays a major role for national bibliographic control. The functions and purpose of national libraries may differ from country to country due to some political agendas. One of the unique privileges of a national library of a country is to receive by law all print and non-print materials produced by the country. With libraries shifting their role from being custodians of collection-based traditional information resources to being providers of access-based digital information resources, the library websites play an important role. Libraries have to disseminate and facilitate access to variety of information to their users through their websites. National libraries around the world maintain their websites which are used to offer a wide range of information, consistent with their wide range of activities, as compared to other types of libraries. So, there are some guidelines in international, national, regional levels for building the various organizational, institutional or any other types of standard websites (Haneefa and Venugopal, 2010). Now the question is how far the national library websites are followed or following the guidelines in building and maintaining their websites? The present work intended to analyse and evaluate the national library websites of Asia. For the present study, the 113 Design Guidelines for Homepage Usability by Jakob Nielsen, 2001 (https://www.nngroup.com/articles/113-design-guidelines-homepage-usability/) and guidelines given by NIC (National Informatics Centre) for Indian Government websites have been taken into consideration as the authentic standard (Nielsen, 2001). From the above said guidelines some parameters have been set and then analyzed and evaluated. Then each of the selected websites has been checked on the basis of each of those selected parameters.

LITERATURE REVIEW

Haneefa K and Venugopal M K (2010) highlighted on the contents and design of national library websites of some Asian countries. Pisanski and Zumer (2006) summarized that European national library web sites do, in fact, have a common core of content and, in large part, follow the design guidelines, but there are still some deviations from the recommendations. National libraries of the economically better developed countries have better web sites in terms of the guidelines followed by them, whereas national libraries of the Eastern and Southern European countries fare slightly worse. Zeinolabedini, Maktabifard and Osareh (2006) studied that the various NLs status in terms of their website quality and performance. Results show that based on this research criteria, Library of Congress website is the most powerful one among world others some NLs websites. In a survey, Smith (1999) compared impact factors of website of Australia and New Zealand national library. After calculating links of these 2 websites, he concluded that Australian NL website is larger and has more in–links rate.

OBJECTIVES

The objectives of the study are as follows:

- This study particularly aims to consolidate the information on national library of Asian countries.
- To analyze the contents of national library websites of Asia countries.
- To identify how far the national library websites are following the standard guidelines.
- To find out the facilities and services provided on the national library websites of Asian countries.
- To suggest measures for the improvement of national library websites.

SCOPE OF THE STUDY

The present study was conducted on the selected national library websites of Asia. This study was restricted within the field of Internet for searching the related websites on national libraries of Asian countries. The study is also restricted within the particular time period i.e. from 01/02/2018 to 30/06/2018. Another decision was taken that the study is restricted within English language based and translation based national library websites only.

In Asia, there are 48 sovereign states, which are member of United Nations in Asia. Also there are 6 Non-United Nation states with limited international recognition, 4 Dependent territory and 2 Special areas of internal sovereignty (http://www.un.org/). The study focused on the homepage of national libraries' websites which are general in nature with their collections, services, e-resources and web 2.0 facilities.

A comprehensive search on the web was conducted and websites were selected for the study from the Asian countries on the basis of following criteria:

- Number of Asian countries or territories which are having national library;
- Number of Asian countries or territories which are having website of national library;

- Number of Asian countries or territories which presented national library website in English language or having comprehensive English version website of national library.
- Major functional university library of some countries treated as national library with legal deposit, which is included in this study.

On the basis of the above mentioned criteria, it was found that 50 Asian countries (including UN & Non-UN members) are having national libraries; out of that only 49 countries are having NL websites. The website of 49 national libraries were examined and observed on different intervals and it was found that out of 49 websites, only 45 are functional national libraries of Asia and have maintained English language website or has translation facilities for conversion into English. So, finally 45 countries were selected.

METHODOLOGY

Data were collected from the home pages and its other related links on the basis of 113 Design Guidelines for Homepage Usability by Jakob Nielsen, 2001 (https://www.nngroup.com/articles/113-design-guidelines-homepage-usability/) and guidelines given by NIC (National Informatics Centre) for Indian Government websites. Apart from the above, data were also collected from different documentary sources and other e-resources. In this study, only five main aspects i.e. the homepage information, information about collections, information on e-resources, information on library services and application of Web 2.0 of the 45 selected national library websites of Asian countries were analysed.

In order to analyse and evaluate the websites of national libraries in Asia, some usability checklists were compiled on the basis of above mentioned guidelines. All these guidelines are modified according to the features and characteristics of national library websites. These checklists were used for the evaluation of the selected websites of national libraries in Asia. Each feature included in the checklist was giving two weightage i.e. one (1), if a particular feature is present on the website and zero (0), if it is not available. For example if National library of India has a window title then it got one point and if it does not have window title then it scores zero point.

ANALYSIS OF THE CONTENTS OF NATIONAL LIBRARY WEBSITES

The checklist designed for the study includes following ten headings under main aspect "homepage information", which started from Aspect-1A to Aspect-1J according to order mentioned below. Ten major aspects were further analysed from checklist's data.

Some other checklists for this study are presented through Aspect-2, 3, 4 and 5. These four aspects actually represent remaining four major aspects, which are analysed in this study also from checklist's data. Collected data are analysed according to above mentioned headings in the following few paragraphs.

Aspect-1A: General Information from Homepage

A library website's homepage or any other type of website's homepage is the main gate of entrance of the virtual visit of a library or other organization. The website homepage should highlight to their user (or customer) about the name and other general information without any delay. A library website's homepage or any other type of website's homepage is the main gate of entrance of the virtual visit of a library or other organization. The website homepage should highlight to their user (or customer) about the name and other general information without any delay. For that the name of the library and its logo should be inserted on the website at a noticeable location so that it can catch first attention when users enter a particular website. In this study the position of name and logo of the selected NL websites of Asian countries were analyzed and found that in most of the national libraries i.e. 35 out of 45 (77.77%), that name and logo of the library are present at the upper left corner of the website. Rest of the national libraries i.e. 10 (22.23%) could not fulfill the parameter. The size of library's name at the website of Singapore, Maldives, Jordon, Japan, Iraq, Iran, Cyprus and China was found small. In the website of Uzbekistan there was not any type of name and logo of library. The selected parameter "About us" of the website gives users brief information about the institution and its various activities. Almost all the selected national libraries, 44 (98%) provided "About us" link on the homepage of the website. There was no about us option in the website of Syria. Some national libraries used different naming terms for heading the "About us" section like 'About me', 'About library' etc. In parallel with "About us" another parameter "Administrative board/structure" of libraries is provided by 19 i.e. 42.22% out of selected NL websites. And 26 NL websites i.e. 57.78% presented their site without "Administrative board/structure" information. All the selected websites (45) of Asian national libraries' provided "Contact Us" information. The information element in the "Contact Us" was different from library to library. Majority of websites provided only complete physical address and email address. In relation with contact information, the "Feedback" parameter provides by 91.11% national library websites (41). "Copyright" information is provided by 40 (88.88%) national library websites and remaining 5 library websites (11.12%) did not provide copyright information. With the copyright information "Date of updation" was mentioned in only 9 (20%) NL websites. There was no update date mentioned in the rest 80% i.e. 36 NL websites. The parameter 'FAQ" is fulfilled by only 35.55% (16) NL websites out of 45 websites. The remaining 29 NL websites presented their websites without FAQ for their users.

Background information through their "History" parameter is provided by 40 (88.88%) NL websites and remaining 5 libraries did not provide information on "History" of their NL.

Information regarding "Library hours" is provided by 25 (55.55%) national library websites and rest 20 (44.45%) did not represent their "Library hours". Similarly "Library map" is provided by only 8 (17.77%) websites and it is not mentioned in the remaining 82.23% (37 NL) websites; "Library tour" parameter is fulfilled by 9 (20%) websites and rest 80% (36 NL) has not; "Membership information" is provided by 25 (55.55%) NL websites and 20 websites did not provide membership details; parameter "Location map" is covered by only 16 (35.55%) NL websites and 29 websites did not have it. Quite good number of NL websites, 35 (77.77%) highlighted their "Goal & Mission" and remaining 10 library websites did not highlight that. "Forthcoming news and events" menu is presented by 37 NL websites and rest 17.78% (8) websites did not provide such information. Sitemap is an important feature of websites. This "Sitemap" is provided by only half of the selected national library websites i.e. 23 websites (51.11%). Other 22 (48.89%) websites did not provide sitemap. Another issue was that, most of the NLs (41 or 91.11%) under the selected libraries provided their websites in more than one language.

Aspect-1B: Features of the URLs of the Homepage

A website URL provides some significant features. Recall value is a one of the significant features of them. Among the selected national library websites of Asian countries (45), it was found that 51.11% (23) websites had a simple and memorable URL. Generally it did not add any complex code or even 'index.html' after the domain name. On the other hand 48.89% (22) websites used some kind of code after the domain name such as "intex.html", "default.aspx", "page.php", "index.php" etc.

Another feature which has been observed is that the URLs of the websites respond with either both "www.library.com" and "library.com" or URLs of the websites respond with only first one, not without prefix (like 'www'). It was found that quite good number 77.77% (35) of websites responded in both the ways and remaining 22.23% (10) websites did not respond when "www." was removed. Another important aspect is whether the website's URL has country's top level domain or not. National libraries are representing its country in the cyber world so it should use its country's top level domain. In addition to that it has national and international users, so the website domain should be one that distinguishes it from other websites. The analysis of domain name of the websites revealed that 86.66% (39) websites were using country's top level domain name and only 13.34% (6) websites were using other domain names such as .org, .com.

Aspect-1C: Features of the Window Title of the Website Homepage

Website window title plays very significant role in the retrieval of website via the search engine which is determined by the title tag of each HTML (Hyper Text Markup Language) document. Search engine uses the window title when user searches through search engine. Therefore, it should be as specific as possible and should begin with informative word, usually or generally the name of the library. Among the selected national library websites of Asian countries, it has been showed that all the websites provide window title to the homepage except National library of Uzbekistan. These window titles sometimes were the name of national libraries or as per their country's language or any other departmental name of particular country. Sometimes window titles begin with the term "Welcome" or "Homepage," which is not wrong or unethical but it does not separate site information. This analysis revealed that some national libraries like National library of Brunei used; window title entitled, "Perpustakaan Brunei Darussalam"; National library of Jordan used the window title entitled "Home: Department of the National library", National library of Saudi Arabia used the term "KFNL", National library of Oman used the window title entitled "The Sultan Qaboos University Library" etc. which were not started with the name of the library. Out of 45 national libraries, 35 (77.77%) NL websites started with user friendly names and rest of the national libraries 10 (22.23%) started the window title with the name of others title. From another perspective an analysis showed that all the websites did not include the top- level domain name such as .com, .in, .pk etc. in their window title.

Aspect-1D: Features of Date and Time

National libraries all over the world have international users so it should use international time zone on its website and those (NL websites) using local time zone must use standard abbreviation. The study revealed that just more than half 57.78% (26) websites were using international time zone and rest of 42.22% (19) websites were using local time zone on their website. In case of the clarification of date on the website, it's better to spell out the month, instead of writing it in number form. In this study it was found that almost half 48.89% (22) websites fulfill this criterion and 51.11% (23) websites were not following this criterion. Both (using number to show the month and spell out the month) formats of date was found on 17.39% websites. It is better to follow only one pattern of date to avoid any type of ambiguity.

Aspect-1E: Features of the Content Writing

There is a basic difference between writing for a webpage and writing for a printed source. On the web, users are basically scanning the web pages instead of reading. Libraries have their own terminology but general users are not familiar with these technical LIS terms. It is necessary to use user friendly language or define the technical terms wherever necessary. All the selected national libraries of Asian countries frequently used technical terms on their websites such as OPAC, online database, digital resources, e-resources, union catalogue etc. But there was one library i.e. the National library of Indonesia which provided link to the dictionary of the "library term" used on the website. Other than that various parameters should be maintained by any type of websites. One parameter "avoid unnecessary uppercase letter" is maintained by most of the, 41 (91.11%) NL websites and rest 8.89% (4) websites are just opposite and used uppercase letter some times. In order to emphasize the importance of categories or links, web designers repeat the links on the homepage but this act actually reduces their impact. A homepage of the website is the index page; every piece of information should be linked from it and for that redundancy should be avoided on the homepage. The analysis highlighted that almost all 44 (97.77%) websites had no repetition of content on the homepage. In this analysis it was found that just over half number of websites, 24 (53.33%) avoid single item categories and single item bulleted list. In this study Aspect-1E highlighted that 51.11% (23) national libraries' websites in Asia spell out abbreviations and acronyms to provide immediate and easy understanding to all users, especially for person, using a screen reader but 48.89% (22) NL websites did not spell out the abbreviations and acronyms. The common abbreviations and acronyms used on the websites were RSS, UN, ISBN, ISNN, CIP, IFLA, OPAC and ISO. Another issue found in this study was that, all the selected NL websites (45) did not use spaces and punctuations appropriately for emphasis.

Aspect-1F: Navigation Features of the Website

The primary purpose of a homepage is to facilitate good navigation for easy and user friendly movement.

There is a need to put proper attention on navigation in the process of designing of a website so that navigation would be able to reveal all the content of the website. Labeling of links on the homepage should be as specific and brief as possible. It should start with informative word. In this study analysis shows that 82.22% (37) websites followed this norm. Remaining 8 (17.78%) did not follow this criterion. For example, the headings on the homepage of National library of India were entitled 'More about National library', 'View Recently Digital Books' etc. and in the same way on the website of National library of Iraq heading were entitled 'NLA publication', 'NLA Department', 'NLA Services' etc. The collected data reveals that 33 (73.33%) websites provided link to homepage from each webpage of the website and remaining 26.67% (12) websites did not follow this criterion. Under this study majority of national libraries i.e. 93.33 (42) websites did not use generic instruction such as "Click Here" and fulfill the parameter except the National libraries of Bangladesh, Bahrin and Brunei. It was found that instead of underlining or colouring, some national libraries i.e. 11 (24.45%) used the word 'Links', 'Quick Links', 'Necessary Links', 'Pages' and 'Navigation Menu' etc. to show the list of links on the homepage. This thing should be avoided by the national libraries for increasing the usability of the websites. 'The primary navigation area in a highly noticeable place' this parameter covered by 88.88% (40) NL websites and remaining 11.12% (5) websites did not provide such feature. As per standard guideline each website should allow change of link colour to indicate visited status by user. Among the selected websites of national libraries in Asia only 5 national libraries (11.12%) i.e. National library of China, Japan, Iraq, India and Nepal allowed the link colours to show visited and not visited status. Others 88.88% (40) did not support that. A link to the homepage on the homepage is clickable, users will inevitably click on it and wonder if the page has indeed changed. This analysis shows that 40% (18) NL websites provided an active link to the homepage on the homepage and rest 60% (27) was just opposite.

Aspect-1G: Searching Feature of the Website

The primary aim of the users on the website is to find the information as early as possible. In this study an attempt was made to analyse all search features of the national libraries' websites of Asian countries. Within all NL websites, 24.45% (11) websites did not have a way to search the website. Remaining 75.55% (34) websites had the search facility. "Provision of an input box instead of just giving them a link to search" parameter is matched by 77.77% (35) websites with the search box on the homepage of the website. Remaining 22.23% (10) did not support it. In the search box, 30 plus characters should be visible so that a user can see the entire search. And also they can modify it during the search process. Only 28.88% (13) websites support this benchmark via wide search box. Rest of the national libraries 32 (71.12%) had the search box below 20 characters i.e. small. Advance search option is provided by only 17.77% (8) national libraries and remaining 82.23% (37) did not provided advance search. The data reveals that among the 77.77% (35) websites which provided site search option on its website. Among them five libraries label the search box with the heading 'Search' instead of using a "Search" button to the right of the box. The thirty three (73.33%) websites of national libraries did not label the search area, in its place they provided the search button on the right of the box and rest websites were just opposite.

Aspect-1H: Graphics and Animation of the Website

In general meaningful explanatory text description must be provided for images, graphics and other non-text elements in any type of website. For that <ALT> HTML tag must be defined in the coding of the webpage.

Sometimes browser takes time to load a webpage, that time it is helpful because text loading is faster than images or non-text materials. The data shows that 55.55% (25) websites satisfied this measure and 44.45% (20) websites did not fulfill this criterion of usability. Any watermarks graphics or images decrease the visibility and add no value to documents. Almost all the websites 93.33% (42) under study avoided the use of watermarks on the homepage of the websites and remaining 3 (6.66%) websites including Saudi Arabia, Singapore and UAE used it. Generally vertical scrolling is normal attribute and it was habituated with computer hardware i.e. mouse but horizontal scrolling is not good feature of a website. In this study maximum of the websites 95.55% (43) avoided horizontal scrolling and rest of the two websites used it. Use of high-contrast text and background colors supports the legibility of websites. Out of selected websites 80% (36) websites fulfilled it and rest 20% (90) websites did not fulfill it. To specifically highlight the content or to bring in notice the particular information to the users, most of the time website content is animated. But there should be some mechanism in the hand of uses to control the animated work like scrolling and blinking of the content. Animation of critical elements of the page, such as the logo, tag line, or main headline is not a good choice for users. Only 26.67% (12) websites maintained it.

Aspect-1I: News and Press Releases

It is important to make news stories and press releases effective on website's homepage. This applies to either the organization's news that presented on homepage, or any news that website delivers as a content. Headlines and decks should actually give users outline information, before clicking through to the real information. Headlines should be succinct, yet descriptive, to give maximum information in as few words as possible. The data shows that 88.88% (40) websites satisfied this measure and 11.12% (5) websites did not fulfill this criterion of usability. Under the parameter, Link headlines, rather than the deck, to the full news story data reveals that 80% (36) national library websites fulfill the criterion and rest 20% (9) did not fulfill.

Aspect-1J: Popup Windows and Advertising

In general, it is best to show site content immediately. Intermediary screens are rarely necessary and keep users from getting to the main site content. The intermediate pages might confuse some users into not recognizing the "real" homepage. Advertisement also creates various confusions. The parameter, "Keep external ads (ads for companies other than your own) as small and discreet as possible relative to your core homepage content" is satisfied by 97.77% (44) NL websites and rest 2.23% (1) did not satisfy this parameter. The intermediate pages i.e. pop-up windows might confuse some users into not recognizing the "real" homepage. So, the parameter avoids pop-up window, fulfilled by 95.55% (43) NL websites and 4.45% (2) websites did not satisfy it.

Aspect-2: Information about Library Collection

All the NL websites provide their detailed collection. The type and scope of their presentation varies from website to website with general to more detailed information. Table- 6.2 shows that the information about the collection like 'Books', 'periodicals', 'Audio visual documents', 'Maps', 'CD/DVD', 'Rare collection', 'Regional collection', 'Micro documents' etc. on the websites. In this study it was found that all the NL websites (45) provided details of their book collection and all the NL websites provided their regional collection on their websites. Information on foreign collection was provided by 75.55% (34) national library websites and remaining 24.45% (11) websites like Armenia, Brunei, Iraq, Iran etc. did not provide that information. The rare collection of the national library is provided by 39 (86.66%) websites among the selected websites. Remaining 13.34% (6) websites did not provide information about rare collections. Different kinds of special collection information are provided by 60% (27) national library websites and rest 40% did not. Very few of NL websites provided the details of children's information i.e. 13 (28.88%) and remaining 32 (71.12%) did not highlight information on children's collections. The children's collections are available in the NL websites of Brunei, Japan, Singapore, UAE, Macao etc. Almost the half, 23 (51.11%) national libraries among the selected national library websites have links to new additions on their websites and others 22(48.89%) did not represent such information. Information on audio video materials and CD/DVD were provided on the 33 (73.33%) NL websites and 26.67% (12) websites did not fulfill this. Almost all the website 43 (95.55%) among the selected websites provided details of the subscribed journals or periodicals and the same number of websites (43) provided information about newspapers on their websites. The information on microform collections of the national libraries were provided by almost 26 (57.78%) national libraries in their websites and was not provided in remaining 19 (42.22%) websites. Twenty five (55.55%) national library websites were represented by their music collection information for users. A good number of national library websites i.e. 38 (84.44%) provided details of maps and 7 (15.56%) were present without information on map collections in their respective websites. A quite good number of websites presented the detailed information of their manuscripts (75.55%) and photograph (71.11%) collections. Information about manuscripts and photographs in the national library websites were provided by 34 and 32 websites respectively. In the remaining numbers i.e. 11 (24.45%) and 13 (28.89%) respectively, there were no information about manuscripts and photographs. The national libraries generally act as legal depositories in order to collect each and every published document in the country and about the country also. The large number of national libraries i.e. 41 (91.11%) provided information on legal deposit. Less than half numbers of national libraries from selected national library websites provided details of the dissertations 20 (44.55%) in their websites and 18 (40%) websites gave details of on-going projects. The remaining 55.55% (25) and 60% (27) websites did not satisfy this criterion regarding the information on thesis/dissertations and projects.

Aspect-3: Information on E-resources

Present era is known as the age of ICT or the digital age. To create effective and efficient library website, it must include electronic resources including e-journals, e-databases, e-books etc. This study revealed that a good number of the libraries 28 (62.62%) provided links to e-books in their websites and rest 17 (37.78%) websites were not like that. National library websites of China, Iran, Israel, Georgia etc. provided links to e-books. Very good number of NL websites provided links to e-journals [35 (77.77%)] and e-databases [40 (88.88%)] on their websites and there are websites without information about e-journals and e-databases i.e. 10 (22.23%) and 5 (1.12%) respectively. For example, information on the e-journals subscribed and maintained by the national libraries of China, Japan, Malaysia, Singapore, India, Iran etc. are reflected in their websites. A good number of websites i.e. 39 (86.66%) provided information on Intranet facility in their library. Very few number of national library websites i.e. 11 (24.45%) highlighted the information about online exhibition or seminars. The website of national library of China and other ten websites reflected information on online exhibition or seminars.

Aspect-4: Infromation about Library Services

Aspect-4 depicts various type of services which are available via the national library websites. Majority of library websites 41(91.11%) provided links to their OPAC in their websites and remaining 4 (8.89%) had no OPAC service. Almost half number of selected libraries provided the service of Inter Library Loan i.e. 26 (57.78%) and Document Delivery Services [29 (64.45%)] on their websites. Inter Library Loan service and DDS links were not provided on the 19 (42.22%) and 16 (35.55%) websites respectively. All the NL websites (45) provided links to referenence services and 30 (66.66%) websites provided bibliographic services in their websites and rest 15 (33.34%) were without information on bibliographic service. Reprographic service was specified by the 25 (55.55%) national library websites and was not specified by remaining 20 (44.45%) websites. Information on indexing services was provided by only 12 (26.67) websites. Rest 73.33% (33) websites were without information on indexing service. Good number of national libraries provided the details of services to researchers in their websites. Thirty national library websites (66.66%) reflected information about the services to the researchers via their websites and other 15 were without any information. Information regarding the preservation and conservation of rare and early printed documents was represented by most of the NL websites i.e. 43 (95.55%).

Aspect-5: Application of Web 2.0 Technology

The term Web 2.0 is a boom of the present time. To find out the application of Web 2.0 in the national library websites by using following keywords such as blog, podcast, vodcast, chat, tagging, RSS, ask librarian, virtual reference, Twitter and Facebook. Among 45 national libraries, 19 (42.22%) national libraries were using RSS application on their websites and rest 26 (57.78%) did not have RSS feed. Among the selected websites only two websites were using Atom service. Other popular Web 2.0 tools are social networking site (SNS), blog and microblog. Only 9 (20%) and 17 (37.78%) national library websites were using blog and microblog for communication and remaining 36 (80%) and 28 (62.22%) websites were without blog and microblog. Among the 45 national libraries, 33 (73.33%) national libraries were using social networking site. Podcast/vodcast is used only by 2 national libraries. Instant messaging (IM) can be used as a virtual reference service but out of 45 national libraries only 9 (20%) provided this on their websites. For sharing photos of events, historical moment's etc. only 12 national libraries were using this feature.

SUMMARY OF FINDINGS

The present study NL websites of Asian countries have been evaluated through five main aspects with 14 broad areas. According to the result, the websites followed some of the selected parameters and did not follow rest of those. Fourteen (14) areas and under 14 areas 100 parameters had been considered in total. When a websites satisfied a parameter, score 1 (one) was assigned for that and when did not satisfy a parameter, score 0 (zero) was assigned for that. So after checking through every parameter, a website scored a certain value which was indeed the summation of 1s (ones). It was finally tried to assign a status to each website. The NL websites were evaluated through such parameters, which made the websites more accessible, qualitative and user centric in implementing them. Thus, it was good for the NL websites to implement as much parameters as possible. So, the scores were converted into grade and then all the NL websites were divided into four levels of grade. The score of each websites and scale division of grade were set as follows.

IF Score e" 80 Grade is "A++"

IF Score e" 60 and < 80 Grade is "A"

IF Score e" 40 and < 60 Grade is "B"

IF Score < 40 Grade is "C"

Depending on this equations the score status of individual NL websites are as follows:

Table 6.2. Score Status of Individual NL Website of Asian Countries

SL No	Total Score 100 (From Aspect 1A – 1J, 2, 3, 4 & 5) Score Distribution of Aspects (Out of individual points i.e. mentioned within brackets)															Total Score & Grade	
	A	B	C	D	E	F	G	H	I	J	K	L	M	N		Total Score	Grade
1	Armenia	12	3	2	1	3	4	3	5	1	2	6	3	10	2	**57**	**B**
2	Azerbaijan	12	1	2	1	3	5	0	4	2	2	13	4	9	1	**59**	**B**
3	Bahrain	5	0	1	1	3	2	4	4	1	2	12	3	5	1	**44**	**B**
4	Bangladesh	10	3	2	0	5	2	4	4	1	2	13	2	9	1	**58**	**B**
5	Bhutan	10	3	2	1	4	5	1	5	2	2	10	2	6	1	**54**	**B**
6	Brunei	11	3	1	1	4	1	4	4	0	2	8	2	10	2	**53**	**B**
7	Cambodia	7	3	1	1	3	6	3	5	2	2	10	2	9	1	**55**	**B**
8	China	13	3	2	1	3	6	4	4	2	2	14	5	12	2	**73**	**A**
9	Cyprus	14	1	1	1	3	4	4	5	2	2	10	3	10	0	**60**	**A**
10	Georgia	12	2	2	2	5	4	3	5	2	2	10	4	11	2	**66**	**A**
11	HongKong	16	2	1	2	4	5	4	3	2	2	17	5	15	4	**82**	**A++**
12	India	14	3	2	1	5	7	0	5	2	2	15	4	11	0	**71**	**A**
13	Indonesia	6	1	2	2	5	4	2	2	2	2	13	4	9	3	**57**	**B**
14	Iran	10	3	2	1	3	4	4	5	2	2	11	3	9	0	**59**	**B**
15	Iraq	9	1	2	1	3	7	3	4	1	2	7	2	4	1	**47**	**B**
16	Israel	14	3	2	2	5	6	4	4	2	2	12	5	14	7	**82**	**A++**

17	Japan	12	3	2	1	4	6	3	5	2	2	15	4	17	4	**80**	**A++**
18	Jordon	12	2	1	1	4	5	5	4	2	1	11	4	12	1	**55**	**B**
19	Kazakhstan	10	2	2	1	3	5	3	3	2	2	6	5	11	3	**58**	**B**
20	Kuwait	9	2	2	1	5	5	3	4	2	2	9	3	8	3	**58**	**B**
21	Kyrgyzstan	6	2	2	1	3	3	0	4	0	2	12	4	11	2	**54**	**B**
22	Laos	10	1	2	0	5	4	0	5	1	2	11	4	10	1	**56**	**B**
23	Lebanon	10	2	2	0	5	4	3	4	2	2	12	3	10	4	**63**	**A**
24	Macao	14	2	2	1	4	6	4	4	2	2	15	5	15	2	**78**	**A**
25	Malaysia	12	2	2	2	4	5	3	3	2	2	12	5	13	6	**73**	**A**
26	Maldives	12	2	2	1	4	5	0	4	0	2	8	3	7	2	**52**	**B**
27	Myanmar	6	2	2	2	5	3	0	4	1	2	15	4	11	4	**61**	**A**
28	Mongolia	10	2	2	1	4	6	3	3	2	2	10	0	11	3	**59**	**B**
29	Nepal	9	3	2	1	4	6	3	4	1	2	12	0	11	0	**58**	**B**
30	Oman	12	1	2	1	4	5	5	2	2	1	10	4	11	3	**63**	**A**
31	Pakistan	12	3	2	1	4	6	2	4	2	2	12	0	11	0	**61**	**A**
32	Philippines	11	1	2	1	4	5	0	5	2	2	13	0	10	1	**57**	**B**
33	Qatar	11	3	2	1	4	5	4	5	2	2	16	4	11	4	**74**	**A**
34	SaudiArabia	11	2	1	1	5	4	4	2	2	2	13	5	13	4	**69**	**A**
35	Singapore	15	3	1	1	4	5	3	3	2	1	14	4	14	7	**77**	**A**
36	Korea South	14	3	2	1	5	4	5	4	2	2	16	5	14	5	**82**	**A++**
37	Sri Lanka	12	2	2	0	5	5	0	4	2	2	16	4	15	1	**70**	**A**
38	Syria	8	2	2	0	3	5	3	4	2	2	13	4	7	0	**55**	**B**

39 Taiwan	17	2	2	1	4	6	3	5	2	2	11	4	13	3	**76**	**A**
40 Thailand	11	2	2	1	4	5	3	4	2	2	12	4	10	3	**65**	**A**
41 Timor-Leste	9	2	2	1	4	2	3	4	2	2	5	0	5	1	**42**	**B**
42 Turkey	14	1	2	1	2	4	3	4	1	2	15	4	15	2	**70**	**A**
43 UAE	14	1	1	1	3	3	3	2	2	2	10	4	11	6	**63**	**A**
44 Uzbekistan	14	3	0	1	4	6	4	4	2	2	15	5	15	1	**76**	**A**
45 Vietnam	15	3	2	2	4	5	0	5	2	2	15	5	14	2	**76**	**A**

Note : A = Name of the National library (Website); B = Aspect-1A(18); C = Aspect-1B(3); D = Aspect-1C(2); E = Aspect-1D(2); F = Aspect-1E(5); G = Aspect-1F(7); H = Aspect-1G(5); I = Aspect-1H(5); J = Aspect-1I(2); K = Aspect-1J(2); L = Aspect-T-2(17); M = Aspect-3(5); N = Aspect-4(18); O = Aspect-5(9)

Table 6.2 represents the status of individual NL website of different countries of Asia. This above table has also been summarized to know which status contains what amount of score (number and grade). The results are highlighted below.

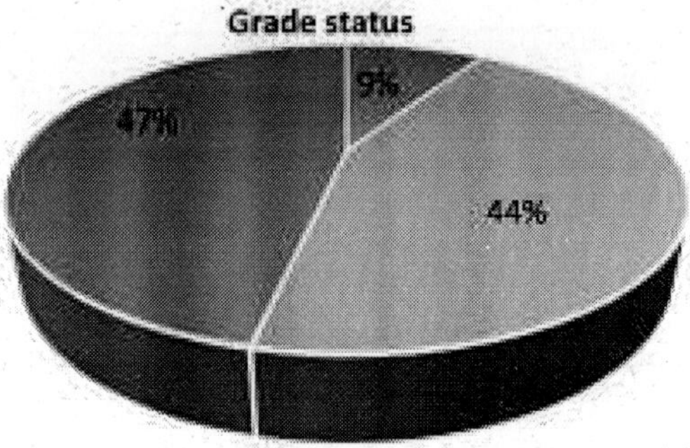

Fig. 6.1. Grade Status of NL Websites

The above figure 8.1 (Pie chart) shows that 9% selected NL websites had fallen in the status of "Grade A+", 44% had fallen in "Grade A", 47% had fallen in "Grade B" and not any website had fallen in "Grade C'.

SUGGESTIONS

- The library name and logo of the library should be visible enough and placed at the most noticeable location on the homepage of the website. The best position for it is the top left corner of the website.
- Website is the gateway of any library or other organizations in this age of ICT. Websites of national libraries should have simple and memorable URL. It should work both with 'www' and without the 'www'.
- National library websites should use country's top level domain name to show its identity at international or global level.
- Homepage or even each webpage of the website should have a simple window title. Title should begin with an informative word i.e. the name of the library.

- Link to "About Us" section should be available on the homepage which should contain comprehensive information about the library including brief history and its different activities. One standard word should be followed for its labeling.
- One uniform pattern of date and month should be followed throughout the website. Month should be spelled out rather than using number.
- "Contact Us" option should include with full physical or postal address, e-mail address, map of the location.
- FAQ and the contact detail of each section and the directory of library staff according to administrative structure should be available.
- National library's website should provide archive of the past events according to particular specific arrangement.
- National library's website contents should use user friendly language instead of library terminology on the website and should provide clear description wherever use of technical language is done, that is mandatory.
- There should not be duplication of links on the homepage of the website of national library.
- Used abbreviations and acronyms should be spelled out whenever and wherever required.
- Proper navigational structure should be incorporated into the website so that user moves around the website easily or jump one location to another location.
- Every page of the website should contain a link to the home page and must show the current position of user on the website through path information.
- Standard link colours should be used for differentiate links that have been visited (previously clicked) and those that have not.

- Search features should be provided because it makes the search easy. Search box should be provided on the homepage instead of just providing a link. The width of search box should be as wide so that user can modify its search query easily.
- "ALT" HTML tag should be provided for all the non-textual elements (Like image) on the website.
- National library website should not use scrolling text, marquees, and constant running animations because these are distracting the library users, if using, there should be some manual control in the hand of users.

FURTHER RESEARCH

The limitation of the present evaluative study of the websites of national libraries of Asian countries created the scope of further research in the field. The scope of further research can be stated as follows:

- The evaluation time period was very short of the present study i.e. six months only. So, a much longer time period of evaluation can be applied for such a study which may result in new findings.
- The geographical scope for such study can be extended. It may cover more than one continent.
- Only those parameters have been selected which can access the accessibility, quality and content of the NL websites of Asian countries. The parameters for accessing the security, audit and other such information of the websites may be applied in another study.
- A multidisciplinary approach is also essential for developing automated usability evaluation tools. Further study can be done on that.

REFERENCES

- Bjorneborn, L. & Ingwersen P. (2004). *Towards a basic framework for webometrics.* Available at https://onlinelibrary.wiley.com/doi/10.1002/asi.20077/abstract (accessed June 14 2018).
- Haneefa, K. & AnjanaVenugopal M. K. (2010). Contents of national library websites in Asia: An analysis. *Annals of Library and Information Studies, 57*, 98-108.
- Nielsen, J. (2001). 113 *Design guidelines for homepage usability.* Available at https://www.nngroup.com/articles/113-design-guidelines-homepage-usability/(accessed June 14 2018).
- Noruzi, A. (2005). Web impact factors for Iranian Universities. Available at http://www.webology.ir/2005/v2n1/a11.html (accessed June 7 208).
- Pisanski, J., & Zumer, M. (2006). National library websites in Europe: An analysis. Available at http://www.emeraldinsight.com/doi/pdfplus/10.1108/00330330510610564 (accessed June 14 2018).
- Smith, A. (1999). ANZAC webometrics: exploring Australasian web structures. Available at http://www.csu.edu.au/special/online99/proceedings99/203b.htm(accessed July2 2018).
- Thanuskodi, S. (2012). A webometric analysis of selected Institutes of National Importance Websites in India. *International Journal of Library Science, 1*(1), 13-18.
- Vijayakumar M., Kannappanavar, B. U., & Santosh Kumar K. T. (2012), Webometric analysis of web presence and links of SAARC countries. *DESIDOC Journal of Library &Information Technology,* 32 (1), 70-76.
- Zeinolabedinio, M. H., Maktabifard, L., & Osareh, F. (2006). Collaboration analysis of world national library websites via webometric methods. Available at http://eprints.rclis.org/7439/ (accessed June21 2018).

APPENDIX 1

Table 6.1. Selected National Library Websites

Name of NL Website	*URL*
Armenia	http://www.nla.am/arm/?q=en
Azerbaijan	http://anl.az/new/en/main
Bahrain	https://librarytechnology.org/libraries/library.pl?id=198548
Bangladesh	http://nlb.gov.bd/
Bhutan	http://www.library.gov.bt/
Brunei	https://www.librarybrunei.gov.bn/library/
Cambodia	http://www.khmerica.com/
China	http://www.nlc.cn/newen/
Cyprus	http://www.cypruslibrary.gov.cy/moec/cl/cl.nsf/dmlindex_en/dmlindex_en?opendocument
Georgia	http://www.nplg.gov.ge/eng/home
Hong Kong	https://www.hkpl.gov.hk/en/hkcl/home/index.html
India	http://www.national library.gov.in/
Indonesia	http://perpusnas.go.id/homepage/
Iran	http://www.nlai.ir/
Iraq	http://www.iraqnla-iq.com/site/index.html
Israel	http://web.nli.org.il/sites/nlis/en
Japan	http://www.ndl.go.jp/en/
Jordon	http://www.nl.gov.jo/En/HomePage.aspx
Kazakhstan	https://nlrk.kz/page.php?lang=3
Kuwait	https://www.nlk.gov.kw/historical_background.aspx
Kyrgyzstan	http://www.national libraryofkyrgyzstan.org/
Laos	http://www.national libraryoflaos.org/
Lebanon	http://bnl.gov.lb/English/index.html
Macao	https://www.library.gov.mo/en/
Malaysia	http://www.pnm.gov.my/
Maldives	https://nlm.gov.mv/
Myanmar	http://www.national library.mn/en/
Mongolia	http://www.nlm.gov.mm/
Nepal	http://www.nnl.gov.np/
Oman	https://www.squ.edu.om/libraries/Home

Pakistan	http://www.nlp.gov.pk/
Philippines	http://web.nlp.gov.ph/nlp/
Qatar	http://www.qnl.qa/
Saudi Arabia	http://www.kfnl.gov.sa/Ar/Pages/default.aspx
Singapore	https://www.nlb.gov.sg/
Korea South	http://www.nl.go.kr/english/
Sri Lanka	http://www.natlib.lk/
Syria	http://www.alassad-library.gov.sy/
Taiwan	http://www.nlt.go.th/th/index.php
Thailand	http://www.cultura.gov.tl/en/institution/projects/national -library-and-archives-of-timor-leste
Timor-Leste	http://www.ntl.edu.tw/mp.asp?mp=2
Turkey	http://www.mkutup.gov.tr/en/
UAE	https://www.abudhabi.ae/portal/public/en/homepage
Uzbekistan	http://www.natlib.uz/en
Vietnam	http://nlv.gov.vn/ef/

7
Conclusion

Webometrics research with its different facets has reached a new height in this 21st century. It has its application in various sectors of this information era. This book in its different chapters has revealed those aspects of webometric analysis. Be it the Web Impact Factor analysis or the usage of different features of Search Engine Optimization or the analysis of hyperlinks in designing link topology or even the website content analysis, all these are flagrant with their presence in the five case studies. From the field of education to the field of politics webometric study has its application.

The amalgamation of bibliometric style of investigations with that of the descriptive and social science oriented nature of webometrics is also the watchword of webometrics research in this present era. There is no doubt that webometric techniques will continue to evolve in response to new web developments, seeking to provide valuable descriptive results and perhaps also commercially applicable data mining techniques. Webometrics is potentially able to gather a wide range of evidence of research impact or connections as web is full of enormous amount of information. But lack of quality control regarding web data hints at the fact that webometric results are normally indicative rather than providing robust evidence. Another point is that web data is incomplete in several senses and in arbitrary ways which results into partial reflection of the activities of research in the output of a webometric analysis (Thelwall, 2008). Inspite of many shortcomings in analysing the web centric information webometrics research plays an undeniable role.

REFERENCES

- Thelwall, M. (2008). Bibliometrics to webometrics. *Journal of information science*, *34*(4), 605-621.